THE ART OF HOSTING: YOUR HOLIDAY ENTERTAINING HOW-TO FOR THANKSGIVING, CHRISTMAS, AND FAMILY GATHERINGS

YOUR COMPLETE FAMILY GATHERING COOKBOOK TO HOME ENTERTAINING WITH THANKSGIVING HOSTING TIPS, CHRISTMAS HOSTING ESSENTIALS & CONVERSATION STARTERS THAT SPARK JOY

ELANA HART

Table Of Contents

- Introduction
  - Welcome to Effortless Home Entertaining: How to Host Without the Stress
- Part I: Building Your Hosting Foundation
  - Chapter 1: The Heart of Home Entertaining
  - Chapter 2: Holiday Hosting Essentials Every Beginner Needs
  - Chapter 3: Your Step-by-Step Holiday Hosting Plan
- Part II: Mastering Holiday-Specific Celebrations
  - Chapter 4: Thanksgiving Hosting Tips for a Memorable Meal
  - Chapter 5: Christmas Hosting Essentials: From Décor to Dinner
  - Chapter 6: How to Host a New Year's Eve Party They'll Never Forget
- Part III: Planning, Food & Style Made Easy
  - Chapter 7: Easy Ideas for Year-Round Family Gatherings
  - Chapter 8: Holiday Meal Planning Made Simple
  - Chapter 9: Table Setting and Decorating Ideas That Wow
  - Chapter 10: Drinks, Toasts, and Bar Setups for the Holidays
- Part IV: People, Conversation & Party Dynamics
  - Chapter 11: Conversation Starters and Icebreakers That Actually Work
  - Chapter 12: How to Handle Awkward Guests, Family Drama & Conflict
- Part V: The Entertaining Toolkit
  - Chapter 13: How to End a Party Gracefully (And Keep Guests Smiling)
  - Chapter 14: DIY Hosting Hacks for Last-Minute Magic
  - Chapter 15: Hosting on a Budget: Affordable Celebrations That Shine
- Conclusion
  - Host with Joy, Not Stress: Your New Holiday Hosting Mindset

INTRODUCTION

Welcome to Effortless Home Entertaining: How to Host Without the Stress

Let's start with a familiar scene:
 You're frantically fluffing throw pillows and checking the oven clock. The roast isn't quite done, your guests are due any minute, and the table still looks like a mix of Pinterest and panic. You light a candle and hope the scent distracts from the fact that you forgot to chill the wine. Your playlist isn't queued, your hair isn't brushed, and your heart is racing.
 Sound familiar?
 If you've ever hosted a holiday gathering—or just *thought* about hosting one—you know the internal pressure that comes with wanting everything to go perfectly. But here's the truth no one talks about enough:

You don't have to be perfect to be a great host.
 In fact, the best hosts aren't the ones with the most expensive serving platters or flawless menus. They're the ones who create

spaces where people feel relaxed, welcomed, and truly seen. This book is here to help you become *that* kind of host—the kind who doesn't stress over a burnt pie or mismatched napkins because they're too busy enjoying their own party.

The Art of Hosting is about taking the stress out of holiday entertaining and replacing it with something better: confidence, ease, and connection.

Why Hosting Doesn't Have to Be Overwhelming

Let's bust a few myths right away:

You do **not** need a sprawling dining room, a perfectly curated Pinterest board, or a gourmet cooking degree to host beautifully. You don't need to buy matching wine glasses or cook a five-course meal from scratch. And you definitely don't need to be someone you're not.

You just need to be willing.

Willing to open your home—even if it's a small apartment or a messy kitchen. Willing to gather people—even if they don't all know each other. Willing to lead with presence, not perfection.

True hospitality isn't about impressing people. It's about making them feel comfortable. It's not about how things *look*—it's about how people *feel*. And sometimes, the best conversations happen over paper plates and store-bought pie.

If the idea of hosting feels overwhelming, take a breath. You are not alone. Even seasoned hosts feel pressure sometimes. But with the right tools, a flexible plan, and a little mindset shift, you can host with calm, joy, and confidence—no matter your experience level.

From Perfectionism to Presence

Somewhere along the way, hosting became a performance. The table had to be Instagram-worthy. The menu had to impress. The kitchen had to look like no one had ever actually cooked in it. But here's the thing: **trying to get it all right often means missing what really matters.**

INTRODUCTION

I once hosted a Thanksgiving where nothing went as planned. The turkey took too long, the green beans were limp, and my "signature pie" cracked right down the middle. To top it off, I forgot to buy ice. I was so focused on fixing everything that I barely spoke to my guests for the first hour.

Then something unexpected happened. One of my friends walked into the kitchen, handed me a glass of wine, and said, "You know what? This is perfect." I looked around. People were laughing, kids were playing, and the house smelled like cinnamon and roasted garlic. No one cared about the cracked pie. They cared about being together.

That's when I realized: presence beats perfection. Every time.

From that moment on, I stopped aiming for flawless and started focusing on *being fully there*—with my guests, in my space, enjoying the moment I had created. That's the mindset this book will help you adopt.

I call it the **calm host mindset**: less performance, more peace. Fewer rigid expectations, more room for joy. You'll learn how to let go of hosting anxiety, plan with flexibility, and actually enjoy your own parties.

Let this be your new mantra as you read:
Connection over perfection.

Who This Book Is For

This isn't a book for professionals. It's a book for real people with real lives who want to create gatherings that feel warm, meaningful, and fun—without losing their minds in the process.

First-time hosts:

Hosting your first Thanksgiving or Christmas? Unsure how to plan a meal or seat your guests? I've got you covered—with checklists, timelines, and zero judgment.

Busy families:

Between work, school runs, and soccer practice, finding time to host can feel impossible. This book is packed with shortcuts, swaps, and smart strategies for doing more with less stress.

Seasoned pros:

Already hosting every year but secretly dreading the chaos? Want to freshen things up or simplify the process? You'll find new ideas, inspiration, and maybe even permission to do less.

Everyone in between:

Live in a small apartment? Don't love cooking? Feel awkward making conversation? You're in the right place. Whether you're an introvert, a perfectionist, or someone who just wants to bring people together—you're welcome here.

No matter your background, budget, or floor plan, **you can host beautifully—and enjoy it too.**

How to Use This Book as Your Holiday Entertaining How-To Guide

This book was designed to feel like a trusted friend—one you can flip through for quick inspiration or sit down with when you're planning your next gathering. Whether you're prepping a month in advance or Googling "what to serve last-minute for Thanksgiving," this guide meets you where you are.

It's flexible on purpose.

You can read it cover to cover to build a strong foundation—or jump directly to the chapter that fits your current need.

Here's what you'll find inside:

- **Holiday-specific sections:** Hosting Thanksgiving? Turn to Chapter 4 for stress-free planning, menu ideas, and *Thanksgiving hosting tips* that work in real life. Planning Christmas? Chapter 5 covers *Christmas hosting essentials*from décor to dinner. New Year's Eve? Chapter 6 shows you how to host a celebration your guests will remember all year long.

- **Evergreen hosting tools:** Learn the core elements of great *home entertaining*—from meal planning and signature cocktails to conversation starters, table settings, and conflict-free hosting. These are tools you'll use again and again, no matter the occasion.

- **A Hosting Toolkit at the back:** Need a last-minute checklist? Emergency hosting fix? Budget-saving menu tip? The final chapters include printable planning tools, DIY hacks, and fast reference pages to keep you calm when time is tight.

Dog-ear pages. Write notes in the margins. Fold down corners. Make this book your own. Hosting isn't about getting everything right—it's about finding what works for *you*, and doing it with love.

Final Words of Encouragement

If you've ever thought, "I could never pull off hosting a big holiday," let me tell you something:

You don't need permission to host. You already have everything it takes.

The magic is already there—in your kindness, your thoughtfulness, your desire to bring people together. This book is simply here to help you access it with more ease and less overwhelm.

In the chapters ahead, we'll start by building your foundation: a clear mindset, a flexible plan, and a few smart tricks to make every gathering more joyful. Whether you're hosting your first Friendsgiving or looking to refresh your family traditions, you'll find support, structure, and encouragement on every page.

So grab a warm drink, take a deep breath, and let's begin.

Welcome to the art of hosting—with heart.

PART I: BUILDING YOUR HOSTING FOUNDATION

Before you light a single candle or plan a menu, you need something deeper than décor: a strong foundation. This section is your starting point—where we shift your mindset, define your hosting style, and build the confidence you need to create gatherings that feel good for you and your guests.
You'll learn what really matters when people come together, how to prepare your space with purpose, and how to plan without pressure. Whether you're a first-time host or someone looking to rediscover the joy in entertaining, this is where your journey begins.
Let's lay the groundwork for calm, connected, and confident hosting—starting from the inside out.

1
THE HEART OF HOME ENTERTAINING

Before we dive into menus, décor, or guest lists, let's start with something deeper. Something that matters far more than centerpieces or perfectly browned casseroles.

Let's talk about **why you're hosting in the first place.**

Because the truth is, it's easy to get swept up in the logistics. The grocery lists. The table settings. The three types of stuffing your guests might expect. But hosting isn't really about any of that. At its core, **home entertaining is about creating a space where people feel welcome, seen, and connected**—not just impressed.

What Guests Actually Remember

I want you to think about the best gathering you've ever attended.

Close your eyes for a moment and picture it.

Now, ask yourself: Do you remember what was served? What the napkins looked like? How tidy the bathroom was?

Or do you remember how you *felt*?

Most people can't recall every dish or décor detail, but they *can* recall the laughter around the table. The moment someone told a great story. The warm greeting at the door. The way the room felt safe, fun, and full of life.

That's the kind of experience this book is here to help you create.

When we take the pressure off ourselves to perform—and focus instead on presence—we shift from entertaining to *hospitality*. And that's where the magic happens.

Creating Meaningful Gatherings with Intention

Every great gathering begins with one simple but powerful question:

Why am I hosting this?

It sounds basic, but your answer guides everything—from what you serve to how you set the mood. Are you gathering people to celebrate tradition? To reconnect with friends? To bring comfort in a tough time? Or maybe to start a new ritual of your own?

Hosting with intention gives your event purpose. It turns a dinner into a memory, a brunch into a tradition, and a party into something people will talk about for years.

You don't need to do anything extravagant. Even a simple ritual—like going around the table and sharing what you're grateful for, or playing a song that means something to your group—can transform a casual get-together into something unforgettable.

Why Hospitality Is More Important Than Presentation

Let's be honest: we've all felt the social pressure to host like an influencer. To make our homes look magazine-ready. To create a menu worthy of a cooking show. But here's the truth:

No one is coming over to judge you. They're coming over to be with you.

"Letting go of perfection"

Yes, beautiful details can enhance the experience. But they're not the *heart* of the experience. Your guests want to feel relaxed, welcomed, and at ease—not like they've stepped onto a set where one wrong move might ruin the aesthetic.

I've been to gatherings where everything looked flawless but felt stiff and formal. And I've been to homes where the dishes didn't match, the food came out late, and yet I laughed until I cried and never wanted to leave. I bet you've had that experience too.

Real hospitality says: **"Come as you are. You're safe here."**

That is the atmosphere people remember. That is the gift of a great host.

Small Shifts, Big Impact

Let's shift the question we often ask ourselves before hosting.
Instead of:
"What will they think of me?"
Ask:
"How do I want them to feel?"
This simple change takes you out of performance mode and

places you in a position of generous leadership—one where your presence matters more than your perfection.

Keep these three simple intentions in mind as you host:

1 Make guests feel seen. Greet them warmly. Say their name. Introduce them to someone new.

2 Reduce friction. Think about flow—where people will sit, how they'll grab drinks, where coats will go.

3 Bring joy into the room. Music, laughter, comfort—small touches that say "you're welcome here."

The Takeaway

You don't need matching silverware. You don't need a menu full of new recipes. You don't even need to clean your baseboards (promise).

What you *do* need is a little intention, a little presence, and the willingness to open your space to others—even if it's imperfect.

Hospitality is about connection, not performance.
It's about presence, not perfection.
It's about people, not presentation.

As you move through this book, keep coming back to that truth. Write it on a sticky note. Tape it to your fridge. Let it guide you whenever you feel the pressure creeping in.

Now that we've established the heart of home entertaining, it's time to explore your unique style—and start building a foundation that reflects who *you* are as a host.

Let's get started.

2

HOLIDAY HOSTING ESSENTIALS EVERY BEGINNER NEEDS

If you're just starting out as a host—whether it's your first Thanksgiving, your first time with in-laws, or the first time your home is the "gathering place"—you might be feeling two things at once: **excitement** and **mild panic**.

That's completely normal.

This chapter is here to help you replace that panic with preparation. You'll discover your personal hosting style, learn how to set up your space (yes, even a tiny one!), and stock your home with the tools and mindset you actually need to feel confident.

Discovering Your Unique Hosting Style

Let's begin with this: **you don't need to host like anyone else.**

Not like your mom. Not like your favorite influencer. Not even like your neighbor with the Pinterest-perfect centerpiece.

The best hosts are the ones who bring their own personality into the experience. Maybe you're the "relaxed and rustic" host who lights candles, serves a one-pot meal, and lets people help themselves. Or maybe you're more of the "elegant and intentional" host who plans a full menu and color-coordinated place cards. Both are beautiful. Both work.

Here are a few questions to help uncover your style:
- Do you feel more at ease in a casual, cozy setting or a refined, formal one?
- Do you prefer potlucks and buffet-style meals or plated, sit-down dinners?
- Would you rather cook everything yourself or collaborate with guests?
- Are you energized by larger crowds, or do you thrive with a more intimate group?

No matter where you land, your style should reflect what feels most natural to you—not what looks best online. That's what your guests will respond to most: **authenticity.**

Setting Up Your Space for Comfort and Flow

Let's talk about your space—whether you have a large dining room or a studio apartment with a folding table and couch seating. **You don't need a big home to host beautifully.**

What you *do* need is a little thoughtfulness in how you use your space.

Start with these simple hosting zones:

1 **Welcome Zone:** Where guests enter. A coat rack, a place to drop bags, and a friendly greeting go a long way.

2 **Food & Drink Station:** Set up an easy-to-access spot for snacks, drinks, or self-serve dishes. This prevents bottlenecks in the kitchen and encourages guests to mingle.

3 **Seating & Conversation Area:** Arrange chairs so people can talk comfortably. It doesn't have to be a formal setup—pillows on the floor, benches, even mixing chairs from different rooms works.

Tips for comfort and flow:
- Light a candle or use soft lighting to instantly create warmth
- Play music as guests arrive to set the tone

- Offer a welcome drink or snack right away—it relaxes everyone
- Don't overcrowd your space with décor or excess furniture

Remember: hosting is about people *feeling at ease*, not being impressed by your square footage or design choices.

The Must-Have Tools for Calm, Confident Hosting

Here's the good news: you don't need a registry's worth of equipment to host well.

A few versatile items go a long way:
- Neutral dishware (enough for 6–8 guests is a great start)
- A couple of large serving platters or bowls
- Pitcher for water, cocktails, or iced tea
- Cloth napkins or simple paper ones
- Serving utensils (tongs, ladle, large spoon)
- Wine opener, bottle opener, cork trivet, and a few candles

You also want to keep a few pantry staples on hand that can save you in a pinch:
- Crackers, nuts, and spreads
- A simple frozen appetizer or dessert
- Shelf-stable drinks or sparkling water
- A good playlist ready to go (trust me—it counts as a tool)

And no need to splurge. Use what you have. Mason jars as glasses? Beautiful. Tea towels as napkins? Genius. It's not about matching—it's about making it work.

Mindset Shifts That Change Everything

Let's clear up a major myth:

Being a good host does *not* mean doing everything yourself.

It also doesn't mean everything needs to be homemade, curated, or executed perfectly. You're allowed to:
- Ask guests to bring a dish
- Buy dessert from a bakery
- Use paper plates if that's what works
- Serve pizza with candles and call it a holiday meal (it counts!)

Here are a few mindset mantras to carry with you:
- *"Done is better than perfect."*
- _"This is supposed to be fun."

3
YOUR STEP-BY-STEP HOLIDAY HOSTING PLAN

If hosting feels overwhelming, it's usually not because you're not capable—it's because you're trying to do everything at once.

That changes here.

This chapter will walk you through a clear, flexible, and stress-reducing plan you can follow before any holiday gathering. Whether you're planning weeks in advance or throwing something together quickly, this timeline gives you structure without pressure.

The goal? Help you feel *calm, confident, and prepared*—so you can enjoy your own party just as much as your guests.

Planning with Purpose, Not Pressure

Let's start by acknowledging a truth: planning gets a bad rap.

It can feel rigid or overly structured. But when done well, planning isn't about perfection—it's about *creating space* for presence. When you're not running around frantically the day of, you're able to connect more deeply, laugh more freely, and respond with flexibility when something inevitably goes sideways (because it always does).

This chapter will guide you through:
- A realistic, week-by-week holiday prep timeline
- Simple budgeting strategies
- How to confidently delegate so you don't do it all alone

Let's begin with the timeline.

Your Realistic Holiday Hosting Timeline

This flexible timeline assumes a holiday event about 3–4 weeks away, but you can condense or stretch it as needed. Just like your menu, this plan is something you can season to taste.

3–4 Weeks Out

- **Set your intention.** Ask yourself: *What kind of experience do I want to create?*

Is it cozy and casual? Traditional and elegant? Kid-friendly? Decide the tone now.

- **Make your guest list.** Confirm the date and reach out for RSVPs.
- **Plan your menu style.** Decide whether you'll cook everything, do a potluck, order food, or some combo of the above.
- **Evaluate your space.** Where will people sit, eat, hang out?
- **Inventory your hosting tools.** Count plates, chairs, glasses. Note anything you need to borrow, buy, or rent.
- **Rough out your budget.** More on that in the next section.

2 Weeks Out

- **Finalize your menu.** Choose dishes based on your time, skills, and energy.
- **Assign potluck contributions.** Be specific! ("Can you bring a veggie side for 8?")

- **Order anything that needs delivery.** Table décor, candles, wine, etc.
- **Start light cleaning.** Tidy surfaces and declutter high-traffic areas.
- **Freeze anything that can be made ahead.** Pie crusts, cookie dough, soups, sauces.

1 Week Out
- **Buy non-perishables.** Pantry items, drinks, dry goods.
- **Confirm RSVPs.** Text or email anyone you haven't heard from.
- **Prep any décor.** Make or arrange your centerpiece, fold napkins, polish servingware.
- **Prep audio and ambiance.** Set up your playlist and check your lighting.

2–3 Days Before
- **Do your main grocery run.** Get fresh produce, dairy, and meats.
- **Start prep cooking.** Chop veggies, make sauces, bake pies or desserts.
- **Clean key spaces.** Bathroom, kitchen, entryway, guest area.
- **Set up any rentals or extra furniture.**

Day Before
- **Cook major dishes.** Mashed potatoes, stuffing, desserts—anything that reheats well.
- **Set the table.** Or at least set it aside, ready to go.
- **Prep your drink station.** Chill wine, slice citrus, set out glasses and mixers.
- **Final walkthrough.** Do a calm sweep of your space with a cup of tea in hand.

. . .

Day Of

- **Prep last-minute items.** Roasts, dressings, warming sides.
- **Start music and candles early.** Create atmosphere before the doorbell rings.
- **Get dressed before guests arrive.** Trust me—it's a game changer.
- **Build in 15 minutes of quiet.** Sit, breathe, drink something warm or bubbly.
- **Welcome your guests.** Be present. Be proud. Let the celebration begin.

Budgeting and Planning with Intention

Let's talk money.

Holiday hosting can become expensive fast—but it doesn't have to. Setting a budget is less about limitation and more about intentionality. Where do you want your time and energy to go? What matters most to *you*?

Your Budget Buckets:
1 Food & Drink – Usually the biggest category
2 Décor – Tableware, candles, flowers, etc.
3 Extras – Printed menus, games, party favors

Party planning budget buckets

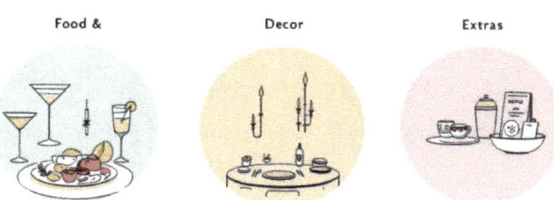

The Good / Better / Best Method
- **Good:** Inexpensive or homemade options that work great (paper napkins, potluck dishes)
- **Better:** Small upgrades (cloth napkins, seasonal centerpieces)
- **Best:** Optional splurges (wine pairings, catering, pro cleaning service)

Money-Saving Tips:
- Keep the menu focused and seasonal
- Reuse or repurpose décor
- Batch cocktails instead of a full bar
- Borrow folding chairs or serveware from friends
- Prioritize what guests will *feel* over what they'll *see*

Planning with intention helps you spend where it matters—and skip what doesn't.

Delegation Strategies That Save Your Sanity

Here's your permission slip to **stop doing it all yourself.**

Not only is delegation practical, it actually makes hosting *more fun*—for you *and* your guests. People like to feel useful, and giving them a clear role creates shared ownership of the experience.

What to Delegate:
- Food dishes (appetizers, sides, desserts)
- Drinks (a friend brings wine, someone else makes a cocktail)
- Setup help (someone arranges chairs or sets the table)
- Clean-up roles (assign discreetly or trade favors)

How to Delegate Well:
- Be specific: "Could you bring a salad that serves 6?" works better than "Bring whatever."
- Use shared notes or group texts to stay organized
- Let people choose based on their strengths: "Would you rather bring dessert or help with setup?"
- Accept help even if it's not your style—people are offering love in their own way

Remember: **a host is a leader, not a martyr.**

Your Hosting Plan in a Nutshell

To recap:

- Start with a timeline. Spread out your prep and avoid last-minute chaos.
- Plan with your budget and values in mind.
- Ask for help early and often. Hosting is a team sport.
- Use the Hosting Toolkit in the back of this book for templates, checklists, and cheat sheets.

You're not planning for perfection. You're planning for peace, presence, and connection.

PART II: MASTERING HOLIDAY-SPECIFIC CELEBRATIONS

Now that you've built a solid hosting foundation, it's time to put it into action—one holiday at a time.

In this section, we'll dive into the heart of seasonal entertaining: Thanksgiving, Christmas, New Year's, and other meaningful gatherings throughout the year. You'll find realistic timelines, flexible menu ideas, decorating shortcuts, and ways to create moments that feel special—without the stress. Each chapter is packed with practical tips and thoughtful touches to help you celebrate in a way that reflects your values, your time, and your energy. Whether you're hosting your first Thanksgiving or refreshing your annual traditions, these guides will help you approach every holiday with confidence and calm.

Let the celebrations begin—on your terms.

4
THANKSGIVING HOSTING TIPS FOR A MEMORABLE MEAL

Thanksgiving is one of the most beloved holidays—and also one of the most stressful to host.

Unlike birthdays or casual dinners, Thanksgiving comes with **expectations**, both spoken and unspoken: the perfect turkey, the passed-down pie recipe, the seating of relatives who may not get along. It's a holiday rich in tradition, emotion, and food—but that richness can also bring pressure.

This chapter is here to change that.

Whether you're hosting your very first Thanksgiving or you've been leading the charge for years, you'll find simple, flexible, and heartfelt tips to help you create a gathering that's meaningful, manageable, and completely your own.

Why Thanksgiving Matters (and Can Feel Overwhelming)

Thanksgiving is more than a meal—it's a memory in the making. It's where stories are told, traditions are passed down, and sometimes, tensions are quietly simmering along with the gravy.

For many, Thanksgiving brings joy. For others, it can also bring stress, family conflict, or grief. Maybe you're dealing with a changing family dynamic. Maybe you're trying to blend new traditions with old ones. Or maybe you're simply trying to cook a meal for more people than your oven thinks is reasonable.

Whatever your Thanksgiving looks like, one thing is true: **you do not have to do it all—or do it perfectly.**

Your mashed potatoes don't have to be whipped just right. Your turkey doesn't have to be centerfold-worthy. And you don't need to make *everything* from scratch.

Instead, let's reset the goal:

Not picture-perfect.

Just personal, peaceful, and meaningful.

That's the Thanksgiving people remember—and the one they'll want to come back to year after year.

. . .

Choosing Your Menu: Classic, Modern, or Somewhere in Between

When it comes to Thanksgiving, the menu often feels sacred—but it doesn't have to be set in stone. You get to decide what kind of experience you want to create, whether it's a traditional spread, a plant-based feast, or a cozy meal for four.

Classic Thanksgiving Menu Essentials

These are the tried-and-true staples most people expect (or crave):

- Roast turkey
- Stuffing or dressing
- Mashed potatoes with gravy
- Green beans or a vegetable side
- Cranberry sauce
- Pumpkin or pecan pie

These dishes are comforting, familiar, and crowd-pleasing for a reason. But that doesn't mean they need to be complicated.

Simple ways to serve them with ease:

- **Turkey:** Roast a breast instead of a whole bird for smaller groups
- **Stuffing:** Use a mix or bake it the day before, then reheat with broth
- **Mashed potatoes:** Keep warm in a slow cooker
- **Green beans:** Sauté with garlic and lemon instead of doing a full casserole
- **Cranberry sauce:** Buy it, dress it up with orange zest or cinnamon
- **Pies:** Make one, buy the rest

Let go of the idea that everything has to be handmade to be meaningful. A well-loved shortcut is still a loving gesture.

Modern (or Flexible) Menu Variations

Maybe traditional isn't your style. Or maybe you want to put a fresh spin on the holiday. Here are some ways to modernize your menu while still keeping it festive and flavorful:

Vegetarian or Plant-Based Thanksgiving Ideas:
- Stuffed acorn squash or roasted cauliflower "steaks"
- Lentil loaf or mushroom Wellington
- Vegan gravy and dairy-free mashed potatoes
- Coconut milk pumpkin pie

Global or International Flavors:
- Moroccan-spiced sweet potatoes
- Cranberry chutney with ginger and garam masala
- Caribbean rice and peas
- Korean-style roasted Brussels sprouts

Mix-and-Match Traditions:
- Roast chicken or salmon instead of turkey
- Cornbread stuffing with jalapeños
- Cranberry salsa over cream cheese with crackers
- Wild rice pilaf instead of mashed potatoes

The key is to keep flavors bold, dishes colorful, and the process relaxed.

Dietary-Friendly Options

Today's Thanksgiving tables are more diverse than ever—gluten-free, dairy-free, vegan, nut-free, and more. Don't let this intimidate you. A little planning makes a big difference.

Tips for Inclusive Menus:
- Ask guests ahead of time about dietary needs
- Label dishes clearly (consider small tent cards)
- Keep some basics allergen-free (e.g., plain mashed potatoes, olive oil veggies)
- Offer a variety of sides so everyone has a full plate
- Use dairy-free butter and stock where possible for shared dishes

Gracious hosting means making everyone feel welcome—and that includes what's on their plate.

Menu Planning Formula: Keep It Simple

Here's an easy way to build a balanced and satisfying Thanksgiving menu:

1 Main Dish (turkey, chicken, vegetarian entrée)
2–3 Sides (starch, veggie, stuffing)
Bread or rolls
1–2 Desserts (pie, crisp, or something chocolate)
Optional: Welcome appetizer and signature drink

This framework keeps you from overcommitting while still feeling generous and abundant.

Bonus Ideas: Crowd-Pleasing Additions

- **Welcome drink:** Apple cider sangria, cranberry fizz, sparkling water with rosemary
- **Simple appetizer:** Cheese board, hummus with crackers, spiced nuts
- **Kid-friendly extras:** Mac & cheese, rolls with jam, mini cupcakes

Thanksgiving doesn't need to be elaborate to be exceptional. It just needs to feel thoughtful, inclusive, and full of heart. The next step? Making that meal happen with less stress and more joy—starting in your kitchen.

In the next section, we'll talk about time-saving cooking strategies, what you can prep ahead, and how to make Thanksgiving Day feel manageable instead of manic.

Time-Saving Kitchen Tricks & Make-Ahead Magic

If there's one thing seasoned Thanksgiving hosts learn over time, it's this: **the more you can prep ahead, the more relaxed you'll be on the big day.**

Thanksgiving doesn't have to be a 10-hour cooking marathon with you stuck in the kitchen while everyone else enjoys themselves. With a few clever strategies, you can *actually enjoy* the holiday too.

Start Early: What to Do in Advance

Here's what you can do 2–3 days before:

- **Make sauces**: cranberry, gravy base, vinaigrettes
- **Bake pies or chill dough**: many pies are even better the next day
- **Chop and prep vegetables**: onions, celery, carrots, herbs—store them in zip-top bags or containers

- **Assemble casseroles**: green bean, sweet potato, stuffing (just bake day-of)
- **Set your table**: one less thing to worry about

Tip: Create a cooking schedule and stick it on your fridge. It reduces decision fatigue and helps you delegate.

Oven-Space Hacks

One of the biggest Thanksgiving challenges? Everything needs the oven—and there's only one.

Here's how to make it work:
- Use **slow cookers** for mashed potatoes, stuffing, or warm dips
- Keep **vegetables on the stovetop**—roast some ahead and sauté others last-minute
- Reheat dishes in a **toaster oven** or **air fryer** in batches
- **Serve in waves**: the main doesn't have to come out with every side at once
- Keep food warm in **foil-wrapped dishes in a cooler**—yes, really! It holds heat surprisingly well

Store-Bought, Dressed Up

You don't have to make everything from scratch. Say it with me: **store-bought is not cheating.**

Some brilliant store-bought shortcuts:
- **Rolls** from the bakery + herbed butter
- **Boxed stuffing** upgraded with sautéed veggies and fresh herbs
- **Canned cranberry sauce** cut into slices and topped with orange zest
- **Pumpkin pie** from the store, topped with cinnamon whipped cream and nutmeg

A great host knows when to let go of the extra steps and focus on what really matters.

If You Only Have 2 Hours…

Life happens. If you're pressed for time or planning last-minute, stick to this simple plan:
- **Roast a turkey breast or rotisserie chicken**
- **Make one starch** (instant mashed potatoes or boxed stuffing)
- **Sauté a green vegetable**
- **Buy a pie and a bottle of wine**
- **Light candles, put on music, and serve it with love**

That's a complete Thanksgiving. Truly.

Setting the Table: Simple Décor, Big Impact

Once your menu is set and your prep is underway, it's time to create the space where everyone will gather. And here's the good news: **you don't need expensive dishes or professional styling to create a beautiful Thanksgiving table.**

A few thoughtful touches can transform even the most casual space into something warm, welcoming, and festive.

Easy Table Décor Ideas

Use what you have—and add a seasonal twist:
- **Natural elements**: mini pumpkins, pinecones, apples, sprigs of rosemary, eucalyptus
- **Candles**: tall tapers or tea lights instantly create ambiance
- **Textiles**: a scarf or throw blanket can double as a table runner
- **Layered textures**: mix wood, linen, and ceramic for an organic look

You don't need matching anything—mismatched plates and vintage glassware can be just as charming.

DIY Centerpieces (No Florist Required)

You don't have to spend a dime on flowers. Try one of these:
- A wooden bowl filled with citrus fruits and herbs
- A few mason jars with seasonal branches or dried flowers

- A cutting board with votive candles and mini gourds arranged around it

Bonus: these are easy to remove when it's time to serve food!

Make It Personal

The most memorable tables aren't the fanciest—they're the most thoughtful. Try adding:
- **Handwritten place cards** (with each guest's name and one word of appreciation)
- **Mini gratitude notes** on each plate
- **A shared activity**: leave blank cards or a runner where guests can write what they're thankful for

Small details speak volumes—and show your guests they were considered.

Lighting + Scent = Atmosphere

Don't underestimate the power of soft lighting and a welcoming scent:
- Dim overhead lights and let candles do the heavy lifting
- Simmer apple peels, cinnamon, and cloves on the stove
- Turn on a playlist with warm, instrumental background music

Your table isn't just about the food—it's where connection happens. With just a few simple touches, you can create a space that invites people to slow down and savor the moment.

Creating Connection: Conversation Starters & Gratitude Rituals

A beautiful table and a full menu make for a lovely holiday. But what really makes Thanksgiving memorable? **Moments of genuine connection.**

This section is about moving beyond the small talk and helping your guests—whether they're old friends

or brand-new acquaintances—feel seen, heard, and appreciated. You don't have to be an extrovert or a professional facilitator. A few thoughtful prompts and simple rituals can completely change the tone of your gathering.

Why Conversation Matters More Than the Turkey

The food is what brings people to the table.

The conversation is what makes them stay.

Thanksgiving often includes guests from different generations, backgrounds, and beliefs. This can be beautiful—or a little tense. By gently guiding the conversation, you set the tone. You show people that this isn't just a meal—it's a shared experience.

Easy, Low-Pressure Conversation Starters

These aren't cheesy icebreakers or awkward games. These are warm, open-ended prompts that invite meaningful stories and spark real connection. You can introduce one during dinner, use them as place card prompts, or offer them during dessert.

Try questions like:
- What's one thing you're especially grateful for this year—and why?
- What tradition from your childhood would you love to bring back?
- What's one lesson you learned this year that surprised you?
- Who's someone who made a difference in your life recently?
- What's one dish you look forward to most at Thanksgiving—and what's the story behind it?

If your group is chatty, these will flow naturally. If they're quieter, you can write prompts on slips of paper and let each guest draw one at random.

Gratitude Rituals for Every Table

You don't need a formal script or a long ceremony to make gratitude part of your meal. Here are a few simple, heartfelt ways to bring meaning to your gathering:

1. Pass-the-Pumpkin

Pass a small pumpkin (or any seasonal item) around the table. When someone receives it, they share one thing they're thankful for—then pass it along.

2. Gratitude Jar

Place a jar or bowl in the center of the table with small slips of paper. Ask guests to write something they're grateful for and drop it in. Read them aloud after dinner (anonymously or with names).

3. Thankful Table Runner

Roll out kraft paper or butcher paper as a table runner. Provide markers and encourage guests to write messages of gratitude directly on the table throughout the evening.

4. Kids' Corner Gratitude Game

If you're hosting families, have a craft table where kids can draw or write what they're thankful for on leaves or turkeys to "serve" later. Include their creations in the main table discussion.

Keeping It Real: How to Avoid Awkwardness

You know your guests best. Not everyone will want to participate in a group ritual—and that's okay. Here's how to keep it inclusive and comfortable:

- **Lead by example**: Share your own gratitude first to set the tone
- **Make it optional**: Frame prompts as invitations, not expectations
- **Keep it light**: If someone jokes or deflects, let it go. The goal is connection, not control

Hosting is about making people feel safe—not putting them on the spot.

The Heart of Thanksgiving

When your guests leave, they may remember the pie. They might comment on the table. But what they'll hold onto most is **how they felt at your table**—welcomed, relaxed, and maybe a little more connected to themselves and each other.

And that, more than anything else, is what makes a holiday meal unforgettable.

. . .

By now, you've seen that hosting Thanksgiving doesn't require a degree in culinary arts or a Pinterest-perfect home. What it does *require is heart, a bit of planning, and the willingness to let go of perfection in favor of presence.*

Let Go of the Pressure

Thanksgiving is a celebration, not a performance. If the turkey is dry or the pie burns, it's still a success if your guests feel seen, nourished, and welcomed. Your warmth is more important than your whipped cream peaks.

Play to Your Strengths

If cooking is your thing, great—go all in. If it's not, lean into store-bought help, potlucks, or no-cook menus. If decorating makes you light up, focus your energy there. If it doesn't, light some candles and call it good.

There's no "right" way to host—there's only the *right-for-you* way.

Remember: You Set the Tone

As the host, your energy is contagious. If you're calm, your guests will be too. If you're stressed, they'll feel that. Give yourself permission to enjoy your own party. Take five minutes before guests arrive to sit down, take a breath, and step into gratitude.

Even if everything isn't finished—*you're ready.*

. . .

Don't Be Afraid to Start Small

You don't have to host a 20-person feast to be a Thanksgiving host. A cozy dinner for four or a brunch with a few friends absolutely counts. In fact, some of the most meaningful holidays happen around the smallest tables.

Your Hosting Reminder

You don't need to impress people. You need to make them feel like they belong.

That's what makes Thanksgiving beautiful.

5
CHRISTMAS HOSTING ESSENTIALS — FROM DÉCOR TO DINNER

Christmas holds a special kind of magic. It's a season of warmth, wonder, and togetherness—but it also comes wrapped in pressure. The desire to create a meaningful, picture-perfect celebration can quickly spiral into overwhelm, especially when you're the host.

This chapter is your permission slip to simplify.

Whether you're hosting a formal dinner, a cozy brunch, a tree-trimming night, or a joyful gathering with kids running through the halls, Christmas doesn't have to be complicated to be beautiful. The heart of it all is ambiance, connection, and presence.

Let's look at how to host the holidays with soul—not stress.

The Heart of a Holiday Home: Festive Ambiance Without the Fuss

Forget the Instagram-perfect trees and elaborate table spreads. Real Christmas magic comes from creating a space that feels **inviting, relaxed, and full of heart.**

The most memorable holiday gatherings don't happen in catalog-worthy homes. They happen where people feel welcome. Where lights are low, music is playing, something good is cooking, and the air feels alive with togetherness.

Let's reframe what it means to create a "festive" home.

Hosting tip: A joyful atmosphere doesn't require a themed party or designer decorations. It just requires a little intention.

Reframing Holiday Hosting: From Grand to Glowing

You do not need:
- A 12-foot tree
- Matching ornaments
- Coordinated wrapping paper
- A snow machine

What you *do* need is warmth. And warmth can be created through **ambiance—not abundance**.

Your goal is to awaken the senses, not the spending habits.

. . .

The Five-Senses Guide to Holiday Ambiance

When in doubt, focus on these five elements:

Sight – Soft, Warm Lighting & Simple Décor

- Dim overhead lights and use table or string lights
- Light candles in clusters (LEDs work too!)
- Skip elaborate centerpieces—try a bowl of ornaments, evergreen sprigs, or pinecones
- Use gold or metallic accents to reflect light and create shimmer without effort

Sound – Let the Music Set the Mood

- Curate three go-to playlists:
  - Instrumental/classical (for meals)
  - Nostalgic holiday classics (Frank Sinatra, Nat King Cole)
  - Upbeat tunes (for gift swaps or cookie decorating)
- Use music to shift the energy of the evening as needed

Scent – Set the Holiday Mood in the Air

- Simmer pot: cinnamon sticks, orange peel, cloves, and rosemary
- Unscented candles for ambiance + a few scented ones placed strategically
- Hang fresh garlands or wreaths—pine brings an instant holiday smell

Touch – Cozy Layers Everywhere

- Add blankets to seating areas
- Use fabric napkins, woven table runners, or velvet ribbon for texture
- Set out fuzzy socks or slippers for guests if you're hosting a casual evening

Taste – Comforting, Festive Flavors

- Keep food simple but satisfying—peppermint hot chocolate, spiced cookies, a warm soup or roast
- Don't forget the drinks: cider, mulled wine, or anything served warm in a mug

. . .

Simple Decor Wins Every Time

You don't need to redecorate your entire home—just sprinkle the season into the spaces where people will gather.

Ideas that work in any size home:
- Fill clear bowls or vases with ornaments
- Drape fairy lights around doorframes, mirrors, or stair railings
- Scatter pine branches across your table or mantle
- Tie ribbon around cloth napkins or hang them from cabinet handles

Pro Tip: Walk through your home and ask, "Where can I add a little glow or green?" That's often all you need.

Use What You Have—Repurpose, Reuse, Layer
- Mason jars = candle holders
- Scarves = table runners
- Grocery store flowers + pine = centerpiece
- Cookie cutters = napkin weights or garland décor

It's not about showing off. It's about showing up—for your guests, for your home, and for the moment.

Hosting Styles for Christmas: Choose Your Experience

There's no one-size-fits-all Christmas gathering. Your holiday can be as formal or relaxed as you want it to be. The secret is to design a celebration that fits your energy, space, and guest list—not someone else's expectations.

Start by asking yourself:
- What kind of gathering feels fun to *me*?
- How much time, energy, and space do I have this year?
- What would make my guests feel relaxed and included?

Let your answers guide your approach.

Choose a Hosting Format That Works for You

Here are a few common styles to consider:

Formal Holiday Dinner
- Best for smaller groups (6–10 people)
- Multi-course meal or buffet
- Candlelight, place settings, seated toasts
- Ideal for Christmas Eve or Christmas night

Casual Brunch
- Great for mixed-age guests, families, or the day after Christmas
- Think quiches, pastries, fruit, coffee, and bubbly
- Can be potluck-style or easily prepped in advance
- Warm and welcoming without being high-effort

Cookie Swap or Cocoa Bar
- Kid-friendly, low-cost, and fun
- Ask guests to bring a dozen cookies to share
- Set up a table with mugs, hot cocoa, marshmallows, and peppermint sticks
- Great for afternoon or early evening

Potluck or Open House
- Low-pressure and communal
- Set a timeframe (e.g., 3–6 p.m.) for guests to drop in
- Keep food self-serve: crockpot chili, snack boards, drinks station
- Less structured = more mingling and ease

Time-Based Ideas to Match Your Schedule
Christmas Eve Candlelight Gathering
- Small group, reflective energy
- Serve light bites or dessert only
- Add a moment of silence, a toast, or a meaningful reading

Morning-After Brunch
- Perfect for lower-key hosting
- Let people arrive in pajamas or slippers
- Offer leftover-friendly or easy-to-assemble food

Kid-Focused Afternoon Gathering
- Include crafts, games, or ornament decorating
- Put on a holiday movie in the background
- Serve snacks that are festive but low-maintenance

Make Hosting Feel Like a Joy, Not a Job

The biggest holiday hosting mistake? Trying to do too much, too fast, for too many people.

Give yourself permission to scale down, simplify, and say no to what doesn't serve you this season.

Remember:
- You don't have to cook everything
- You don't have to host everyone
- You don't have to recreate past holidays to make this one meaningful

Your joy is the secret ingredient to any successful celebration. Protect it.

Low-Stress Meals and Signature Sips

Food is often the heart of any holiday gathering—but it doesn't have to be the source of your stress. Whether you're planning a full dinner or a simple grazing table, the goal is the same: feed your guests with warmth, not overwhelm.

This section helps you plan easy, crowd-pleasing meals and festive drinks that can be made ahead, served simply, and enjoyed by all.

Stress-Free Meal Planning

Let's start with a mantra: **one main, two sides, one dessert.** That's really all you need. Anything more is bonus.

Here are a few flexible formats based on your hosting style:

A Classic Holiday Dinner
- **Main:** Baked ham, roast chicken, or a hearty vegetarian wellington
- **Sides:** Roasted potatoes, maple-glazed carrots, green beans almondine
- **Bread:** Store-bought rolls with herbed butter
- **Dessert:** Pie, trifle, or even store-bought cake topped with whipped cream and berries

Time-saving tip: Roasts are forgiving, can be made ahead, and smell amazing while they cook. Let them do the heavy lifting.

Brunch Gathering
- **Main:** Egg bake or strata (prep the night before!)
- **Sides:** Fruit salad, pastry platter, or pre-sliced bread with spreads
- **Drinks:** Coffee, tea, orange juice, and mimosas

Pro move: Buy a bakery box and transfer everything to trays—instant charm with zero effort.

Grazing-Style or Potluck
- **Main:** Cheese and charcuterie board with crackers, spreads, and nuts
- **Warm dish:** Crockpot soup or meatballs
- **Extras:** Veggie platter, hummus, olives, deviled eggs
- **Dessert:** Cookies, chocolates, or a build-your-own sundae bar

Hosting hack: Use butcher paper or a large cutting board to build your food station—easy setup, easy cleanup.

Vegetarian or Plant-Based Menu
- **Main:** Stuffed squash, lentil loaf, mushroom risotto
- **Sides:** Roasted Brussels sprouts, wild rice salad, cranberry-orange couscous
- **Dessert:** Apple crisp, vegan chocolate cake, or spiced baked pears

Many traditional sides can be made plant-based with a few swaps—and your guests may not even notice.

Signature Sips: Cocktails & Mocktails

Drinks don't need to be complicated to be special. A signature cocktail or festive punch can make your gathering feel instantly elevated—without the need for a full bar setup.

. . .

Cocktail Ideas

- **Cranberry Fizz:** Cranberry juice, vodka, splash of club soda, rosemary sprig
- **Mulled Wine:** Red wine, orange slices, cloves, cinnamon sticks (simmer in slow cooker)
- **Spiked Apple Cider:** Warm apple cider with bourbon or dark rum

Make it easy: Mix one batch ahead of time and let guests serve themselves.

Mocktail & Kid-Friendly Options

- **Sparkling Pomegranate Punch:** Pomegranate juice, lime, sparkling water, mint
- **Holiday Lemonade:** Lemonade + rosemary + frozen cranberries for color

- **Cocoa Bar:** Hot chocolate, whipped cream, crushed candy canes, marshmallows

Pro tip: Use a thermos or carafe to keep drinks warm and cozy throughout the event.

Self-Serve Drink Station Setup
- 1–2 signature beverages (pre-mixed or bottled)
- Non-alcoholic options (sparkling water, juice, soda)
- Cups, garnishes (citrus, herbs), napkins, labels
- A festive tray or bar cart to keep it tidy and fun

It's not about how much you serve—it's about how effortlessly you offer it.

Your food doesn't have to be fancy. Your drinks don't have to be elaborate. When served with heart and simplicity, even the humblest meal becomes something worth celebrating.

Thoughtful, Low-Pressure Gift-Giving

Gifts are often a joyful part of the holiday season—but they can also become a source of stress, financial strain, or awkwardness for hosts and guests alike. That's why the best approach to holiday gift-giving as a host is this: **thoughtful, optional, and low-pressure.**

Whether you want to include gifting in your gathering or gently skip it, this section will help you do it with clarity and care.

Setting the Tone Around Gifts

As the host, you get to set expectations. Clear, kind communication is key—especially if you're gathering people with different traditions or budgets.

. . .

Consider stating upfront in your invitation:
- "No gifts, just your presence is perfect."
- "Let's do a fun $10 white elephant if you'd like to participate."
- "Bring a homemade treat to share instead of a traditional gift."

This takes the guesswork out for guests and prevents the dreaded "I brought something and no one else did" situation.

Group Gifting Ideas That Are Fun and Flexible

1. Secret Santa (Simplified)
- Set a budget (e.g., $20)
- Use a name-drawing app or pull names ahead of time
- Add a twist: each gift must be locally made, homemade, or under a theme (cozy, books, food)

2. White Elephant Gift Exchange
- Everyone brings a wrapped, anonymous gift
- Go around the circle drawing numbers and choosing gifts (or "stealing" someone else's)

- Keep it fun with gag gifts, kitchen gadgets, or dollar store treasures

3. Grab Bag Gifting
- Fill a basket with small wrapped items (tea, candles, candy, socks)
- Each guest chooses one randomly as they leave

4. Experience-Based Gifts
- Have each guest write down a favorite book, movie, or podcast to recommend
- Create a "holiday inspiration jar" that guests can pull ideas from

5. DIY Gift Station
- Set up a table with supplies for guests to make something together: ornament kits, cookie-in-a-jar jars, or hand-stamped gift tags
- This becomes both an activity *and* a takeaway gift

Hosting Tip: Keep a Few Extras on Hand

Someone might bring an unexpected gift—and it's always nice to have a little something to give in return.

Ideas for easy, affordable backup gifts:
- Mini candles
- Hot cocoa packets in a festive mug
- A bag of homemade cookies
- Small jars of jam or honey
- Scented hand lotion or bath salts
- Gift cards (coffee shops, bookstores)

Wrap these simply and keep them in a basket by the door with a bow or tag. If you don't use them? They're great last-minute stocking stuffers for friends or neighbors.

Make Wrapping Easy and Enjoyable

If you love wrapping gifts, go all out—get the kraft paper, twine, and sprigs of pine. But if you *don't* enjoy it, simplify:
- Use gift bags (reuse them if possible!)
- Pre-label gifts with tags to avoid confusion
- Set up a mini "wrapping station" with tape, scissors, tags, and bags to streamline the process

Want to turn it into a gathering? Host a **wrapping night** where everyone brings their gifts and you wrap together while sipping something festive.

Giving Without the Gift

Gifts don't always have to be physical. Sometimes the most meaningful "gift" is a moment of connection, a shared laugh, or a simple thank-you.

Ideas for non-material gestures:
- A heartfelt toast or compliment
- A handwritten card left at each place setting
- A small shared ritual—lighting a candle together, exchanging favorite holiday memories
- A "gratitude wall" where guests write down something they're thankful for

These moments linger far longer than any sweater ever could.

Gift-Giving, Simplified

The most appreciated gifts aren't the fanciest—they're the most thoughtful.

As a host, you set the tone. By offering low-pressure, creative options and making everyone feel considered, you can turn gift-giving into something joyful, not stressful.

Inclusive Holiday Traditions & Activities

Christmas gatherings come in all shapes, sizes, and belief

systems. Some guests arrive carrying decades of cherished traditions. Others may be celebrating their first holiday in a new country, facing grief, or navigating complex family dynamics. As a host, your role isn't to force one version of "holiday spirit" on everyone—it's to create a space where *all* feel included, respected, and welcomed.

This section focuses on how to gently honor the season while keeping your gathering **inclusive, flexible, and meaningful for everyone** at the table.

Welcoming All Backgrounds, Beliefs & Experiences

Start by recognizing that not everyone celebrates Christmas the same way—or at all. Your guests may be from different faiths, cultures, family structures, or emotional seasons. Acknowledging this doesn't "dampen" the holiday—it enriches it.

How to create inclusive energy:

- Use open, neutral greetings: *"We're so glad you're here to celebrate with us!"* or *"This is a winter gathering of love and light!"*
- Avoid assuming everyone shares the same spiritual or cultural traditions
- Ask about favorite holiday customs or foods from guests' own upbringings—it opens the door for joyful sharing

Hosting tip: If you're not sure what someone celebrates, ask privately before the gathering. Most people appreciate the sensitivity.

Inclusive Decor & Language

You can create a festive space without leaning into overly religious symbolism unless that's clearly aligned with your guest list.

Try using:

- Winter greenery, candles, pinecones, fairy lights, and cozy textures
- Words like *"joy," "peace," "togetherness,"* or *"light"*

- Music playlists that include secular holiday classics or instrumental versions

If you do want to include a spiritual or religious element (like a prayer, blessing, or song), offer a quiet explanation and make it optional—never expected.

Simple, Heartfelt Activities for Every Age & Vibe

Not everyone loves organized games or crafts—but having *something* optional helps break the ice and build connection. Try low-pressure, high-enjoyment ideas that allow people to opt in without feeling on the spot.

Ornament Decorating Station

- Set out blank wooden ornaments, paint pens, glitter glue, or ribbon
- Guests can decorate and either take them home or hang them on your tree

Hot Cocoa or Cookie Bar
- A self-serve station with toppings (marshmallows, candy canes, whipped cream)
- Add a cookie decorating kit for kids or crafty adults

Holiday Memory Share
- Invite guests to write down or share:

"What's a favorite holiday moment or tradition from your childhood?"

"What's a tradition you'd love to start?"

- Use notecards, a group toast, or a message board

DIY Photo Booth
- Hang a backdrop (wrapping paper, curtain, twinkle lights)
- Provide Santa hats, reindeer ears, or fun props
- Guests can take selfies or polaroids to remember the night

Easy Group Games for All Ages

Keep the energy light, the rules simple, and the laughs coming.

Ideas:
- *White Elephant:* Add a "steal limit" or theme to keep it moving
- *Holiday Charades:* Write clues like "wrapping presents," "building a snowman," or "singing carols"
- *Who Am I?:* Stick a name on each guest's forehead (Rudolph, Buddy the Elf, The Grinch) and have them guess with yes/no questions
- *Name That Tune:* Play snippets of holiday songs—see who guesses first

Bonus Tip: Have one or two prizes for games (think: candle, chocolate bar, ornament)—it makes things feel just a little more special without extra work.

Tradition Ideas to Start or Share

You don't need to follow old traditions if they don't serve you. And you don't need to invent new ones every year. Just choose one or two that create **connection**.

Meaningful, simple traditions to try:

- **Group toast:** Invite each person to raise a glass and share one hope for the new year
- **Candle moment:** Turn off the lights, light one candle each, and go around the table saying something they're grateful for
- **Wish tree or gratitude jar:** Guests write wishes, blessings, or gratitudes and place them in a jar or hang them on a small tree
- **Group playlist:** Ask each guest to submit one favorite holiday song ahead of time; create a shared playlist for the night
- **Charity tie-in:** Collect donations for a local shelter, write cards to seniors, or sponsor a child/family for the holidays

Remember: **It's not the scale of the tradition—it's the feeling it creates.**

Hosting With Heart

Inclusivity isn't about pleasing everyone. It's about making everyone feel seen, safe, and welcomed to show up as they are. When you prioritize kindness, flexibility, and curiosity, your celebration becomes a space where guests don't just attend—they *belong*.

> *Take a breath.*
> *You don't need a mansion, a Michelin star, or a themed tablescape to host a meaningful Christmas.*
> *You only need a space, a few people you care about, and the willingness to be present.*

What Makes a Great Holiday Host?
It's not perfection—it's presence.

Your guests don't remember your folded napkins. They remember how you made them feel.

It's not about doing it all—it's about doing what feels right for you.

Simplify your menu. Delegate gifts. Reuse decor. It all counts.

It's not about tradition for tradition's sake—it's about connection.

If something no longer feels good, change it. If something new feels meaningful, start it.

You don't have to host like anyone else. You just have to host like *you*.

So light the candles. Serve the soup. Laugh when things go sideways. Let go of perfect and lean into joy. Whether this is your first holiday gathering or your fiftieth, you already have everything it takes to create something beautiful.

And the best part? You're just getting started.

6

HOW TO HOST A NEW YEAR'S EVE PARTY THEY'LL NEVER FORGET

New Year's Eve holds a kind of electricity—equal parts celebration and reflection. It marks the closing of a chapter and the quiet anticipation of what's to come. And as a host, you get to decide how that moment feels for your guests.

This chapter is your guide to creating a New Year's event that feels aligned with *you*—whether that means clinking champagne glasses at midnight, hosting a casual brunch on January 1st, or leading a soul-soothing gathering around intention setting and reflection.

Forget pressure. This is about presence. You can host a memorable New Year's gathering that's stylish *and* simple, joyful *and* meaningful.

Choose Your Vibe: Brunch or Evening Bash

Before you write a menu or cue up a playlist, pause and ask yourself one key question:

What kind of energy do I want to begin (or end) the year with?

The answer will shape the format of your gathering—and help you plan with clarity and joy instead of pressure or obligation. Below are three timeless options, each with its own flavor and feel.

Evening Countdown Celebration

This is the classic New Year's Eve experience: music, drinks, sparkly outfits, and a countdown to midnight.

Best for:
- Adults, friend groups, couples
- Teens or older kids who enjoy staying up
- Anyone who loves to dress up, toast with bubbles, and lean into the festive side

Start Time: 8–9 p.m. | **End Time:** After midnight (or whenever your crew is ready)

What to Expect:
- Guests arrive with energy and sparkle
- Dim lighting, upbeat playlists, and drinks flowing
- Some guests may dress in sequins, suits, or theme attire
- A mix of mingling, dancing, games, and sharing intentions for the new year

- Countdown at midnight—classic or creative (more on that later)

Hosting Tip: You don't have to serve a full dinner. A spread of hearty appetizers or a potluck-style table works beautifully. Think grazing boards, sliders, stuffed mushrooms, or a pasta bake guests can scoop out.

Add a signature drink, disposable champagne flutes, and a few noisemakers—and you've got a celebration to remember.

New Year's Day Brunch Gathering (January 1st)

Want something softer and more nourishing? Host your gathering the *morning after*. A New Year's brunch is cozy, restorative, and refreshingly low-pressure.

Best for:
- Families, neighbors, and mixed-age groups
- Guests who prefer calm to chaos
- Hosts who love breakfast foods and cozy vibes

Start Time: 10–11 a.m. | **End Time:** Flexible (aim for 1–2 hours)

What to Expect:
- Guests arrive in relaxed attire—maybe even pajamas
- Coffee brews, soft music plays, and everyone breathes a little easier
- You serve muffins, fruit, egg bakes, and pastries—most of which can be prepped ahead
- A mimosa or juice bar adds fun without fuss
- Reflective or gratitude-centered moments can be easily woven in

Hosting Tip: Add small, thoughtful touches like place cards with intention prompts or mini journals for guests to write in. You'll create a memory that lingers far longer than the food.

Small & Reflective Gathering

This one is for the heart-led hosts who want depth over dazzle. If you're craving connection, stillness, and thoughtful conversation, this format will feel like a balm.

Best for:
- Close friends, soul circles, or couples
- Guests navigating loss, burnout, or big transitions
- Anyone who wants to *feel* the significance of the year's end

Start Time: 6–9 p.m. | **End Time:** Early enough to honor quiet reflection

What to Expect:
- Dimmed lights, flickering candles, and soft background music
- Cozy seating: floor pillows, throw blankets, warm drinks
- Guests bring journals or are offered notebooks at the door
- The group may share reflections on the past year, write down things to release, or set intentions for the new one
- There's no pressure for loud celebration—just presence, meaning, and calm

Hosting Tip: Structure the evening lightly: begin with warm drinks or soup, lead into a brief reflection activity, then invite free conversation. Offer guests the option to stay for a quiet toast or head home early with full hearts.

Each of these formats can be tailored to your unique hosting style and emotional bandwidth. You don't have to do what everyone else is doing—you just have to do what feels *true* to you.

And remember: no matter which version you choose, you are offering your guests something deeply valuable—the chance to pause, gather, and enter the new year feeling seen, nourished, and connected.

Set the Tone: Themes, Countdowns & Playlists

While the food and drinks are important, what guests remember most about a New Year's party is **how they felt**. Was it light-hearted? Intimate? Fun? Reflective? You have the power to set that emotional tone—and it starts with just a few thoughtful choices.

This section is your guide to using *themes, countdowns, and music* to transform a simple gathering into something truly unforgettable.

Fun Theme Ideas (Optional but Festive!)

Themes are not a requirement—but they can bring a little sparkle, structure, and delight to your celebration. The key is to choose something that matches your crowd and comfort level. Go all out if that excites you, or keep it subtle and suggestive.

Here are a few guest-favorite ideas:

Roaring Twenties
- Think art deco, pearls, feathers, jazz, and champagne towers.
- Guests wear glam attire: sequins, tuxedos, vintage flair.
- Add Gatsby-era music or instrumental swing to the playlist.

Pajamas & Prosecco
- Cozy + classy. Encourage guests to come in loungewear, robes, or matching pajamas.
- Serve breakfast-for-dinner bites, mimosas, and sweet treats.
- Set the mood with soft lighting, plush blankets, and a fireplace (real or digital).

Black & White Ball
- A simple, elegant dress code that makes any gathering feel polished.
- Use black and white décor, balloons, and candles for instant cohesion.
- Great for formal or casual groups who like a touch of class.

"New Year, Old School"
- Go nostalgic: choose the '90s, 2000s, or your group's favorite decade.
- Encourage themed outfits (denim, chokers, band tees).
- Play music and serve snacks from the era—Bagel Bites, Capri Suns, or Ring Pops anyone?

Vision Board Night
- For a more mindful crowd, ask guests to bring magazines or printouts.
- Set up stations with scissors, glue, poster boards, and markers.
- Guests can create a visual intention for the year ahead—fun, creative, and deeply personal.

Hosting tip: A theme should inspire—not intimidate. Keep it optional, light, and open to interpretation. Let people participate how they want.

Creative Countdown Ideas

The countdown is the heart of most New Year's Eve parties—but it doesn't have to be a standard TV ball drop. This is your chance to create a moment of **magic or meaning**, depending on your vibe.

Here are several ways to customize your countdown:

. . .

Traditional & Kid-Friendly Countdowns
- **Midnight Countdown**: Turn down the lights, pass out sparklers or confetti poppers, and raise a toast.
- **Early Countdown for Kids**: Celebrate at 9 p.m. or earlier with juice toasts and balloon drops.
- Use a **YouTube countdown timer** or stream a ball drop online if you don't have cable.

For a Meaningful Twist
"Let It Go" Fire Bowl
- Give each guest a slip of paper to write down something they're releasing from the past year.
- Safely burn the slips in a fire-safe bowl or fireplace.
- It's powerful, symbolic, and surprisingly moving.

"Resolution Reveal" Jars

- Have guests anonymously write down a goal, word of the year, or intention.
- Read them aloud at midnight or let guests draw one randomly to inspire them.

Balloon Countdown
- Fill 5–10 balloons with little activities, questions, or dares.
- Label each with an hour and pop them on schedule (e.g., 7:00 – trivia, 8:00 – dance challenge).
- It builds excitement and makes the evening interactive for all ages.

Quiet Ritual Moment

If your group prefers depth over dazzle, skip the noise and instead:
- Dim the lights
- Light a candle together
- Read a favorite quote or poem
- Toast with intention: "To what we learned, to what we're letting go, and to what we're becoming."

It doesn't have to be elaborate to be meaningful.

Party Playlists That Set the Mood

Music is the emotional undercurrent of your event. It fills the silences, sets the pace, and ties the whole experience together. Think of your playlist as the pulse of the party—and plan it in stages.

Arrival & Mingling (Soft & Warm)
- Acoustic covers, lo-fi beats, classic soul, light jazz
- Keeps the vibe open and comfortable as guests settle in

Main Party Time (Energetic & Upbeat)

- Danceable pop, throwbacks, hip-hop, and hits from the past year
- This is your soundtrack for games, movement, and countdown energy

Post-Midnight Wind-Down (Cozy & Nostalgic)
- Classic ballads, indie folk, R&B, or "slow dance" tracks
- Helps transition the energy into calm goodbyes or late-night chats

Pro Tip: Crowdsource Your Soundtrack

Ask guests to send in 1–2 favorite songs from the past year ahead of time. Use them to build a collaborative playlist. It makes everyone feel included and sparks conversation: *"You picked this one? I love it!"*

Use Spotify, Apple Music, or YouTube to build your mix—and don't forget to download it in case your Wi-Fi crashes mid-countdown.

Whether your party ends in a dance circle, a shared toast, or a quiet round of journaling, your tone is what will echo in your guests' memories.

Set it with heart, and it will last well into the new year.

Food & Drink: Flexible, Festive, and Easy

You don't need to be a gourmet chef or spend days in the kitchen to impress your guests. In fact, for New Year's Eve, the **best menus are the most manageable**—light bites, make-ahead favorites, and a few celebratory sips go a long way.

Whether you're hosting a midnight countdown or a mellow January 1st brunch, this section gives you easy, crowd-pleasing ideas to serve food and drinks with style—without stress.

. . .

Evening Bash Menu Ideas

For an evening party, think **handheld, buffet-friendly, and prep-ahead**.

Appetizers & Finger Foods
- Charcuterie board with meats, cheeses, crackers, and fruit
- Stuffed mushrooms or deviled eggs
- Mini sliders or pulled pork sandwiches
- Caprese skewers or cucumber bites with whipped feta
- Spring rolls or dumplings with dipping sauces
- Mini quiches or spanakopita triangles

Hosting tip: Offer at least one vegetarian and one gluten-free option. Label your items if possible—it saves you from fielding a dozen questions during the party!

Hearty Bites for a Longer Night
- Sheet-pan nachos
- Mac-and-cheese cups
- Pasta salad or couscous with roasted veggies
- Soup in small mugs (butternut squash, tomato basil, or chili)

Dessert Table
- Brownie bites, mini cheesecakes, or chocolate-covered strawberries
- Cookies in a variety of flavors (easy to bake or buy!)
- A "sweet bar" with marshmallows, candies, popcorn, and sprinkles

Drinks Station
- Champagne or sparkling wine (don't forget non-alcoholic options!)
- Sparkling cider or mocktails for kids and non-drinkers
- Cocktail pitchers (like sangria, punch, or Moscow mule mix)
- Flavored water or infused ice cubes with mint, berries, or citrus

Make it feel fancy: Add garnishes—citrus slices, frozen cranberries, rosemary sprigs. These small touches turn store-bought drinks into something celebratory.

. . .

New Year's Brunch Menu Ideas

Brunch is a comforting and elegant way to host—especially on January 1st when everyone's energy is slower and more relaxed.

Main Brunch Staples

- Egg casserole or frittata (prep the night before!)
- French toast bake with cinnamon and berries
- Smoked salmon platter with bagels and cream cheese
- Waffles or pancakes with toppings (fruit, syrup, whipped cream)

Pastries & Sides

- Croissants, muffins, and danishes (store-bought works perfectly)
- Seasonal fruit salad or yogurt parfait station
- Roasted breakfast potatoes or hash browns

Drinks

- Coffee and tea bar with flavored creamers, cinnamon sticks, and syrups
- Mimosa station with champagne, orange juice, grapefruit juice, and berries
- Smoothies or fresh juice blends (pineapple-mint, orange-carrot)

Hosting tip: Serve buffet-style so guests can help themselves. Stack plates, glasses, and napkins at the start of the table to keep things flowing.

Special Diets? No Problem

Make your gathering inclusive by including a few easy swaps:

- Gluten-free crackers or cookies
- A dairy-free dip (like hummus or guac)
- Vegan-friendly soup or veggie tray
- Meatless sliders or plant-based nuggets

Ask guests ahead of time if there are any allergies or preferences. Most will appreciate the thought—even if they bring their own.

Make-Ahead = Stress Less

Your future self will thank you for prepping as much as possible the day before:
- Pre-slice vegetables and cheese
- Mix cocktail bases (just add bubbles the day of!)
- Set the table or drink station in advance
- Use slow cookers or warming trays to keep things hot without stress

Hosting Tricks to Elevate the Experience

Ambiance Touches
- Light candles or string lights around the food table
- Label food with hand-written cards or chalkboards
- Use tiered trays and cake stands to add dimension to your table

Toast-Worthy Additions
- Have guests write short toasts or affirmations to share
- Pass out sparklers, noise makers, or custom "cheers" tags for glasses
- Offer a "gratitude shot" before midnight—non-alcoholic, but meaningful

Plan for Clean-Up
- Set out labeled trash/recycling bins
- Use compostable or reusable plates and cups
- Keep a tray or basket nearby for dirty dishes or empties

Pro tip: Stash an extra bin under the table for quick cleanup. You'll thank yourself in the morning.

You don't need a gourmet menu to wow your guests. A thoughtful spread, one special drink, and a little bit of joy behind the scenes is all it takes to make your celebration *deliciously memorable.*

. . .

Create Meaningful Closure and a Fresh Start

New Year's Eve isn't just another party—it's a milestone. Whether your guests are coming off a tough year, a transformative one, or something in between, most people are walking into your home carrying quiet hopes, unspoken reflections, and a desire to feel grounded.

As a host, you have a unique opportunity: to help them close the year with meaning—and begin the next one with intention.

This doesn't mean turning your party into a therapy session. It just means building in simple, heartfelt moments that invite reflection, connection, and hope.

Reflection Prompts to Spark Connection

Many guests appreciate a chance to look back and take stock—but few will do it unless invited. You can offer that invitation in subtle, meaningful ways:

Conversation Cards or Table Prompts
- Place a prompt at each place setting or on a card jar near the drinks
- Let guests choose one to answer aloud or discuss in pairs

Ideas:
- What's one highlight from your year?
- What surprised you about yourself in the last 12 months?
- What was a challenge you overcame?
- Who or what helped you the most this year?

Reflection Station
- Set up a quiet corner with cards, pens, candles, and cozy seating
- Provide a few guiding questions and let guests write or journal
- Optional: a basket to anonymously drop answers if they want to share

. . .

Group Gratitude Share
- Invite each guest (if willing) to say one thing they're grateful for before the countdown
- This works especially well for smaller or more intimate groups

Fresh Start Rituals

Rituals are the glue that makes moments stick. You don't need anything elaborate—just something symbolic and shared.

Here are a few beautiful ways to mark the transition from one year to the next:

Let It Go Fire Bowl
- Guests write down one thing they want to release—fear, guilt, stress, regret
- If safe, burn them in a fireplace or fire-safe bowl
- If indoors, tear them up and toss in a "release jar" for fun dramatic effect

Intention Stones or Cards
- Offer guests smooth stones, notecards, or wooden tokens
- Invite them to write a word for the new year (e.g., "courage," "peace," "create")
- They can keep it in their pocket or leave it in a shared bowl as a symbol of collective energy

Wish Wall or Mirror
- Hang paper stars or sticky notes
- Have guests write a hope, wish, or intention for the new year and stick it up
- Optional: read a few aloud or invite guests to take one home

Group Manifesto
- Tape a large sheet of paper to the wall or use a chalkboard
- Title it: *"What We're Calling In for the New Year"*
- Throughout the night, guests add words, doodles, dreams

. . .

Gifts from the Host (Optional but Memorable)

Small parting gifts can double as reminders of the night—and their own inner clarity.

Easy DIY tokens:
- Mini journals or affirmation cards
- Tea bags with handwritten tags ("Steep into something new")
- A printed quote rolled into a scroll
- A gratitude card they can fill out later
- A small candle or essential oil vial

You can place these by the door as people leave with a sign that says:

"Take a little light into the new year."

A Word on Tone

This kind of reflection doesn't need to be serious or solemn. In fact, the more it feels like a gift rather than a task, the more powerful it will be.

Let people participate in their own way. Some will go deep. Others will stay light. That's okay. You've created the space. That's enough.

"You don't need to lead a ceremony to make a night feel sacred. You just need to give people the chance to feel something real."

Last-Minute Hosting Tips & Encouragement

Even with the best plans, things rarely go exactly as imagined. A playlist won't load. The dip might burn. Someone will show up an hour early or late. And guess what?

It's still going to be wonderful.

This final section offers you real-world hosting wisdom—practical tips to stay calm, prepared, and present in the final hours before your guests arrive, plus the mindset reminders that will keep you grounded through it all.

Quick Last-Minute Prep List

Use this checklist to make the final hour feel calm and focused instead of frantic:

Before Guests Arrive:
- Light candles or turn on cozy lighting
- Set out napkins, cups, and utensils (guests hate hunting)
- Turn on music to set the tone instantly
- Prep the drinks station and chill any bottles
- Put a trash/recycling bin in plain view
- Clear one area for coats, shoes, and bags

Optional Bonus Touches:
- Add fresh greenery or citrus to the sink for a subtle scent
- Place a towel by the door in case of wet shoes or snow
- Write a short welcome note or greeting by the door or drink station

Hosting Hacks to Save Your Sanity

Baskets Are Your Best Friend: Use them to store clutter, extra supplies, or anything you don't want guests to see.

Designate a Music Master: Ask one friend to manage the playlist or transitions so it's one less thing for you to think about.

Stack and Serve: Stack plates, bowls, and utensils where people can help themselves—no need for a formal setting.

Prep for Spills: Keep paper towels, stain wipes, and a damp rag nearby (but out of sight). You'll look like a pro when something inevitably spills.

Build in Buffer Time: If the party starts at 8:00, be "ready" by 7:30—so you have time to breathe, eat something, or change your shirt in peace.

Emotional Check-In for the Host

It's easy to get swept up in the timeline, the decorations, or what didn't get done. But before you open your door, take a moment to ask yourself:

"What do I want my guests to feel when they leave tonight?"

Then let everything else fall behind that goal.

Because here's the truth:
- People will remember the *laughs*, not the layout.
- They'll remember the *hug* you gave them, not the hors d'oeuvres.
- They'll remember feeling *welcomed, included, and seen.*

That's the magic of hosting.

Whether you're celebrating big or small, loud or soft, with friends or family or a mix of both—remember this:

You are not just throwing a party. You are offering a doorway into a fresh start.

Let it be joyful. Let it be real. And don't forget to take a moment just for you—to sip your drink, step outside, breathe in the air, and whisper your own quiet hope for what's next.

Happy New Year, host. You've already made it unforgettable.

7
EASY IDEAS FOR YEAR-ROUND FAMILY GATHERINGS

While holidays like Thanksgiving and Christmas often receive the most attention in conversations around hosting, some of the most meaningful and memorable gatherings happen during the quieter parts of the year. Sunday dinners. Spring brunches. A birthday celebrated with sandwiches on the porch. These are the moments that build family culture, strengthen friendships, and make life feel full.

This chapter is your guide to stress-free, heart-centered hosting throughout the entire year. You don't need a formal occasion or a Pinterest-perfect setup—just a willingness to open your door and create space for connection. We'll explore seasonal events, practical menus, and ideas for celebrating everyday life with intention.

Let's begin with a mindset shift that can change the way you think about entertaining: the beauty of small, consistent gatherings.

Why Small, Consistent Gatherings Matter

For many people, the word "hosting" immediately conjures images of holidays—turkeys, gift wrap, fine china, and crowded dining rooms. But when we limit our hospitality to those moments alone, we miss out on the quiet power of gathering regularly, in simple and accessible ways.

There is something deeply grounding about sharing a table with people you care about—not just when the calendar tells you to, but when your heart does.

Reframing the idea of entertaining means moving away from performance and toward presence. Small, recurring gatherings aren't about spectacle. They're about rhythm. They build relationships over time, creating a sense of safety, belonging, and joy that lasts long after the dishes are cleared.

You don't need an anniversary, holiday, or milestone to justify bringing people together. "Just because" is more than enough. In fact, it's one of the most powerful reasons of all.

Gathering regularly doesn't require grand effort. It could look like:
- A standing Sunday night dinner with family or neighbors
- A monthly lunch swap with coworkers or friends

- An annual spring picnic, even if it's just sandwiches and lemonade
  - Tuesday takeout night where everyone brings a different dish

These small traditions act as emotional anchors in the whirlwind of busy lives. They tell your people, "This is a place you can return to. Here, you belong."

They also make hosting feel lighter and easier. When something becomes routine, it stops being a performance. You can relax into it. You find your flow. And your guests do too.

Quick Tip: Consider keeping a simple gathering journal. This could be a paper notebook or a digital notes app where you record:
- Favorite menus that were easy and well-received
- Themes or activities that sparked connection
- Guest lists for recurring events
- Quotes, memories, or funny moments from each gathering

Not only does this help you stay organized—it becomes a beautiful archive of the community you're building, one meal at a time.

In the next section, we'll explore how to adapt this mindset to seasonal family celebrations like Easter, Fourth of July, birthdays, and more—always with simplicity, flexibility, and heart.

Hosting with Ease for Key Seasonal Celebrations

Certain times of the year come with a built-in opportunity to gather. You don't need to make a big production out of these seasonal events—often, a few thoughtful touches, a well-timed invitation, and a simple meal are all it takes to create a memorable family gathering.

This section will walk you through four key types of seasonal gatherings—spring, summer, birthdays, and recurring Sunday-style dinners—and offer suggestions for hosting each one with minimal stress and maximum warmth.

. . .

Easter (or a Spring Gathering)

Easter often signals the beginning of a new season: longer days, blooming flowers, and a fresh energy in the air. Whether you celebrate the holiday religiously, spiritually, or simply as a seasonal reset, it's a natural opportunity to bring people together.

Vibe: Light, fresh, gentle, colorful.

Menu Suggestions:
- Deviled eggs or egg salad sandwiches
- Vegetable quiche or crustless frittata
- Fresh fruit salad or citrus platters
- Lemon poppy seed muffins, cinnamon rolls, or hot cross buns
- Sparkling water with mint or a light citrus punch

Decor: Use what's already in season. A vase of tulips or daffodils, linen napkins in pastel tones, or even a centerpiece made of dyed eggs. You can also repurpose household items—jam jars as vases, a scarf as a table runner.

Activities:
- For kids: an egg hunt, coloring station, or cookie decorating table
- For adults: a "gratitude garden" where guests write a hope or intention for spring on a paper flower and "plant" it in a shared jar or basket

Keep it easy: Host a brunch buffet where guests can help themselves. Focus on what you can prep the day before (egg bakes, muffins, drinks) and spend the morning welcoming your guests instead of cooking under pressure.

THE ART OF HOSTING: YOUR HOLIDAY ENTERTAINING ... 75

Fourth of July or Summer Barbecues

Independence Day gatherings (or summer get-togethers in general) are all about casual, outdoor fun. They're a chance to stretch out, slow down, and enjoy food that's best eaten with your hands.

Vibe: Casual, playful, warm, nostalgic.

Menu Suggestions:
- Grilled burgers (with veggie options), hot dogs, or skewers
- Corn on the cob, pasta salad, baked beans
- Watermelon slices or berry shortcake
- Iced tea, lemonade, or infused water
- S'mores if you have a fire pit or grill

Decor: Picnic-style. Think checkered tablecloths, mason jars, string lights, and paper lanterns. Let nature do the heavy lifting—set up under a tree, near a garden, or on a deck with a view of the sky.

Activities: • Cornhole, frisbee, water balloons, sidewalk chalk
- Create a "freedom wall" where guests (especially kids) write what freedom means to them
- Distribute glow sticks or sparklers (with safety rules)

Make it inclusive: If guests don't observe the holiday, frame the gathering as a "summer celebration" or "backyard night under the stars." The heart of the event is connection—not patriotism or tradition.

Birthdays (Without the Burnout)

Birthdays can be magical—or overwhelming. They're often loaded with expectation, especially for kids, partners, or milestone years. But they don't have to be expensive or complicated to be meaningful.

Vibe: Personalized, celebratory, simple.

Menu Suggestions:
- The guest of honor's favorite dish or comfort food
- Pizza and salad, tacos and rice, baked mac and cheese
- A signature drink or punch that fits their taste (mocktail or cocktail)
- Store-bought cake dressed up with fruit or candles
- DIY dessert bar: ice cream sundaes, cupcakes, or cookies to decorate

Decor: Focus on one area. A photo collage wall, a "birthday banner," or a decorated dessert table can carry the celebration's energy without requiring a full home transformation.

Activities:
- Create a memory jar: guests write a favorite memory with the birthday person
- "Three wishes": ask each guest to share a wish or toast
- Scavenger hunt or trivia quiz for family birthdays

Hosting Tip: Don't feel like you have to host on the exact day. A birthday brunch, weekend potluck, or weeknight dinner can be just as meaningful (and often more manageable).

Sunday Suppers or Monthly Family Dinners

These are the unsung heroes of family connection. Informal, predictable, and centered around comfort food and conversation, recurring dinners bring stability and rhythm to otherwise hectic lives.

Vibe: Comforting, casual, grounding.

Menu Suggestions:

- Spaghetti night with garlic bread and salad
- Roasted chicken with potatoes and seasonal vegetables
- Taco bar with all the fixings
- Crockpot chili or soup with cornbread
- Dessert: brownies, fruit crisp, or ice cream

Decor: Minimal and familiar. A cloth napkin, a lit candle, or even a playlist in the background can elevate an ordinary table. These dinners are about presence, not presentation.

Structure:
- Make it a standing event—every first Sunday, for example
- Rotate hosting or have each person bring one dish
- Choose a "table question" to spark conversation each time:
  ○ What was your high and low of the week?
  ○ What's something new you learned?
  ○ What are you grateful for right now?

Keep it sacred: Let everyone know it's okay to come as they are. No need to dress up, bring gifts, or stay long. The purpose is simply to reconnect.

These seasonal moments offer the perfect starting point for building your own family traditions—ones that reflect your style, your schedule, and your values. In the next section, we'll dig into menus and flexible food ideas that make year-round hosting feel effortless and rewarding.

Menu Inspiration from Your Family Gathering Cookbook

One of the most intimidating parts of hosting—no matter the time of year—is the question: *What am I going to serve?* Whether you're cooking solo or coordinating a potluck, creating a menu that's simple, satisfying, and flexible can mean the difference between hosting with stress... or with ease.

This section offers a "cookbook within your book"—a practical resource for planning meals that work for many occasions, budgets, and dietary needs. Think of it as your **family gathering go-to menu guide**: comforting, adaptable, and always doable.

The Key: Flexible Format, Familiar Food

There's a reason potlucks, casseroles, and DIY food bars never go out of style—they're easy to prep, simple to scale, and a crowd-pleasing hit. Your menu doesn't need to impress, it needs to work.

Start with this core formula:

1 main dish + 2–3 sides + 1 bread or dip + 1–2 desserts = done.

This formula works whether you're feeding 6 or 26. Let's break it down by category.

Easy, Crowd-Friendly Mains

These dishes are warm, hearty, and can often be made in advance or cooked in bulk:

Baked Pastas
- Lasagna (classic, veggie, or gluten-free versions)
- Baked ziti with sausage and marinara
- Macaroni and cheese with breadcrumb topping

Sheet Pan Dinners
- Chicken thighs with root vegetables and rosemary
- Salmon and green beans with lemon and dill
- Tofu and roasted squash with balsamic glaze

Slow Cooker Favorites
- Pulled pork or BBQ chicken sandwiches
- Turkey chili or veggie chili
- Lentil stew or chicken tortilla soup

Taco Night
- Ground beef, shredded chicken, or plant-based crumbles
- Warm tortillas, rice, beans, and toppings

- Serve buffet-style with bowls of cheese, salsa, avocado, lime, cilantro

Grain or Rice Bowls
- Base of rice, quinoa, couscous, or polenta
- Roasted vegetables, protein of choice, sauce (pesto, tahini, vinaigrette)

Comfort Food Staples
- Meatloaf with mashed potatoes
- Shepherd's pie
- Chicken pot pie

Easy, Seasonal Sides

Pair your main with a few of these easy add-ons, many of which can be made ahead:

Vegetable-Based:
- Roasted broccoli or brussels sprouts
- Glazed carrots with herbs
- Green bean almondine
- Zucchini gratin

Starches:
- Herb-roasted potatoes or sweet potatoes
- Couscous or quinoa salad
- Rice pilaf
- Cornbread or biscuits

Cold Sides:
- Pasta salad with vinaigrette
- Caprese salad with tomatoes and mozzarella
- Chickpea or bean salad
- Coleslaw or simple leafy greens with lemon dressing

Bread, Spreads, & Dips

You don't need to bake from scratch—store-bought works wonderfully when served with warmth and intention.
- French bread with olive oil and sea salt
- Pita with hummus or tzatziki
- Cheese and crackers platter
- Chips and salsa or guacamole
- Dinner rolls with herbed butter

Pro tip: Add a basket of bread and a good dip to any meal and you instantly elevate it.

Simple, Delicious Desserts

You don't need a tiered cake or fancy tart. Here are a few easy desserts that feel special without taking over your prep time.

Make-Ahead Favorites:
- Fruit crisp (apple, berry, or pear) with whipped cream
- Chocolate mousse or pudding cups
- Banana bread or lemon loaf

Tray & Finger Desserts:
- Brownies or blondies cut into squares
- Cookies (classic chocolate chip, oatmeal raisin, sugar)
- Mini cheesecakes in muffin tins
- Rice crispy treats with drizzle or toppings

Interactive Dessert Bars:
- Ice cream bar with toppings
- S'mores station (with small burners or a fire pit)
- Cookie-decorating for kids or themed holidays

Make-Ahead Magic

Whenever possible, choose dishes you can prep in advance—this frees you up to be present with your guests, instead of stuck in the kitchen.

Good make-ahead options:
- Pasta bakes and casseroles (assemble 1 day ahead, bake day-of)
- Soups and stews (better flavor after sitting overnight)
- Cold salads (pasta, couscous, beans)
- Breads and dips (can be chilled and plated the day-of)
- Dessert bars, cookies, loaf cakes

Batch your cooking by task: chop all veggies at once, cook all proteins in one go, label containers, and refrigerate. Hosting becomes *much* easier when 80% is done the day before.

Crowd-Size Planning (Without Overdoing It)

A good rule of thumb for gatherings of 6–10 people:
- 1–2 mains
- 2–3 sides
- 1 bread or dip
- 1–2 desserts
- 1–2 drinks (one alcoholic, one not)

Ask guests to bring one dish or drink, and you'll cut your work in half. Hosting doesn't mean doing everything—it means creating the space and inviting collaboration.

Dietary-Inclusive Options

Even simple meals can be inclusive with a few intentional swaps:

Gluten-Free:
- Serve rice, corn tortillas, potatoes, or naturally GF pasta
- Avoid flour-based thickeners or offer GF bread options

Dairy-Free:
- Use plant-based milks, olive oil, or coconut milk
- Avoid cheese-based casseroles or provide a no-cheese version

Vegan/Vegetarian:
- Offer bean-based or lentil dishes
- Include roasted veggies and hearty grains

- Have plant-based dips and desserts available

Label it with love: Add small chalkboard signs or paper tent cards to identify allergens, and always have water and fruit as backup options.

Hosting doesn't have to mean impressing. It can mean offering comfort. Familiar food, shared stories, a plate of something warm—these are the ingredients of memory.

In the next section, we'll look at how to celebrate life's *everyday* moments—not just the obvious ones—and how to bring intention to even the most casual gathering.

Celebrating Life's Everyday Moments

Not every gathering needs a calendar date or cultural holiday to justify it. In fact, some of the most cherished, memory-making events are sparked by simple instincts: "Let's slow down." "Let's celebrate this small win." "Let's be together—just because."

This section is your reminder that hosting doesn't need a milestone—it needs mindfulness. By honoring the seemingly ordinary, you elevate the rhythm of daily life into something beautiful, connective, and joy-filled.

Let's explore practical, low-pressure ideas for gathering around the quiet and unsung moments that make life rich.

Everyday Celebrations Worth Hosting

These are moments that might otherwise pass quietly, but when marked with presence and simplicity, they become meaningful.

1. Back-to-School Breakfast (or Dinner)

Send your kids—and yourself—into the new school year with intention. Invite neighbors, classmates, or family for a casual meal.

- Serve pancakes, fruit, and coffee/juice

- Add a goal board: "One thing I'm excited for this year…"
- Give out small tokens: lucky pencils, mini notebooks, affirmations

2. First Snow Soup Night

When the first flurries fall, surprise your people with a warm gathering.
- Make a big pot of chili, lentil soup, or potato leek
- Have guests wear cozy clothes or bring slippers
- Offer hot cocoa or cider with whipped cream and cinnamon

3. New Job, New Home, or New Chapter Toast

Whether someone is starting a new job, finishing a degree, or moving in, it deserves acknowledgment.
- Invite 4–6 friends for a toast with bubbly or sparkling juice
- Order takeout and keep it easy
- Go around and share one word of encouragement for the honoree

4. "We Survived the Week" Fridays

Not every week will be victorious. Sometimes surviving is worth celebrating.
- Pick one night a month to unwind with friends or family
- Serve comfort food: pizza, nachos, baked pasta
- Have a "one good thing" moment where everyone shares a small win

5. Seasonal Reset Gathering

Use solstices, equinoxes, or the turn of a new season as a built-in opportunity to pause and reflect.
- Spring: gather for intention-setting or "cleansing" meals (greens, grains, citrus)
- Summer: backyard lunch or bonfire
- Autumn: soup swap or story circle
- Winter: candlelight tea or journaling night

Easy Ways to Make Ordinary Gatherings Feel Special

It doesn't take much. Just one or two thoughtful elements can transform a Tuesday night meal into something memorable.

Light a Candle

Even just one. It signals presence and warmth.

Name the Gathering

Instead of "come over for dinner," try:

- Gratitude Night
- Taco Tuesday Toast
- Sunday Reset Supper
- Cozy Circle

Giving it a name makes it feel intentional.

Add a Shared Moment

This could be:

- A playlist built from everyone's song suggestions
- A group photo (even casual and blurry)
- One question passed around the table
- A toast, no matter how short: "To good food and real friends."

Leave a Token

Send guests home with something small but meaningful:
- A handwritten quote or poem
- A leftover cookie in a napkin
- A pressed flower or bookmark
- A note saying, "You made tonight better."

A Mindset Shift: Gatherings Don't Need to Be Grand

We often put pressure on ourselves to wait until the house is perfect, the schedule is open, or the mood is right. But hosting doesn't have to be a production. It can be a **practice**.

When you gather regularly—even informally—you build community muscle. It becomes easier, more joyful, and more natural. You realize it's not about the perfect meal or moment. It's about showing up for each other in small ways, again and again.

Let your gatherings reflect your life: sometimes polished, sometimes messy, always human.

"Life isn't lived in holidays—it's lived in Tuesday dinners, Saturday lunches, and 15-minute coffee drop-ins. These are the moments worth honoring."

PART III: Planning, Food & Style Made Easy

If the heart of great hosting is presence and connection, then the structure behind it is thoughtful planning.

Part III is where we take everything you've learned about calm, confident hosting—and anchor it in logistics. The food. The table. The drinks. The little touches that elevate a gathering from "nice" to "memorable," without making you feel like you're producing a show.

The truth is, stress often comes not from the hosting itself, but from trying to juggle too many details all at once. This section is here to help you simplify, streamline, and enjoy the process—whether you're cooking for five or fifteen.

Let's take a deep breath—and make the practical parts of hosting feel as meaningful as the rest. Starting with what's often the biggest worry: the food.

8

HOLIDAY MEAL PLANNING MADE SIMPLE

Planning a holiday meal can feel like walking a highwire: you want to impress your guests, feed everyone well, respect food preferences, and still be emotionally present when the doorbell rings. But the truth is, meal planning doesn't have to be a stress-fueled sprint. It can be a clear, calm, and even joyful part of your hosting process—if you approach it with the right mindset and some trusted strategies.

This chapter is your complete guide to building balanced menus, simplifying prep, managing dietary needs, and most importantly, reducing last-minute chaos. Let's take the pressure off and put intention—and a little breathing room—back into your planning.

The Hosting Mindset: Planning with Ease, Not Perfection

The biggest mistake hosts make is equating effort with success. More dishes, more hours, more complexity = better hosting? Not quite. A memorable meal isn't about impressing your guests—it's about nourishing them, connecting with them, and making them feel welcome.

Start by asking:
- What kind of mood do I want to create?
- How much time and energy do I realistically have?
- Which dishes bring me joy to make—and which drain me?

Once you name your boundaries and intentions, you can plan a menu that's both beautiful and doable.

Permission slip:

You don't have to make everything from scratch. Store-bought pie, frozen appetizers, or asking someone else to bring the salad doesn't make you a bad host—it makes you a smart one. Choose ease over ego.

Building a Balanced Menu

A good menu doesn't need to be elaborate—it needs to be well-balanced and filling. You want to offer a mix of flavors and textures, while keeping prep (and clean-up) manageable.

The Formula for Success:

1 Main + 2–3 Sides + 1 Bread or Grain + 1–2 Desserts + 1–2 Drink Options

This structure works for most occasions and scales easily.

Sample Menus

Traditional Thanksgiving Dinner:
- Main: Roasted turkey
- Sides: Mashed potatoes, green bean casserole, cranberry sauce
- Bread: Classic stuffing or dinner rolls
- Dessert: Pumpkin pie and apple crisp
- Drinks: Sparkling water, wine, spiced cider

Christmas Dinner (Modern Twist):
- Main: Glazed ham or lentil loaf
- Sides: Roasted root vegetables, kale salad, wild rice pilaf
- Bread: Sourdough baguette with herbed butter
- Dessert: Chocolate trifle and peppermint bark
- Drinks: Mulled wine, rosemary mocktail

New Year's Brunch:
- Main: Egg bake or shakshuka
- Sides: Fruit platter, roasted breakfast potatoes
- Bread: Croissants or bagels
- Dessert: Lemon loaf and mini muffins
- Drinks: Coffee, tea, mimosas

Inclusive Gathering (Anytime):
- Main: Butternut squash risotto or baked ziti
- Sides: Caesar salad, sautéed green beans, chickpea salad
- Bread: Garlic knots or cornbread
- Dessert: Brownie tray and fruit crisp
- Drinks: Iced tea, citrus spritzer

Remember: not every dish needs to be show-stopping. One standout entrée and solid supporting sides are more than enough.

Prep Strategies That Save Your Sanity

Even a simple menu becomes stressful if it's all done last-minute. Smart prepping helps you pace yourself and actually enjoy your gathering.

What to Do in Advance:

2–3 Days Before:
- Shop for all ingredients
- Chop vegetables

- Make sauces, dips, marinades
- Bake cookies or dessert bars
- Set the table if possible

1 Day Before:
- Assemble casseroles or bakes (refrigerate until ready to cook)
- Prep salads (leave dressing off until serving)
- Make cold drinks or cocktail bases
- Clean the kitchen and empty trash/recycling
- Pre-plate or portion snacks and sides

Day Of:
- Start main dishes (turkey, ham, pasta)
- Reheat sides
- Toss salads, refresh drinks
- Light candles, put on music
- Take 10 minutes to yourself before guests arrive

Storage & Organization Tips:
- Use labeled containers ("For oven," "Serve cold," "Reheat at 4:30")
- Store drinks in coolers or bins if fridge space is tight
- Group items by dish: all stuffing ingredients together, etc.
- Keep your sink empty and dishwasher ready the night before

Navigating Dietary Restrictions & Inclusive Eating

A truly thoughtful host anticipates a range of needs—without making a big deal out of it.

Start by Asking:

In your invite or conversation, include a simple line like:

"Let me know if you have any dietary restrictions—I'd love to make sure everyone's covered!"

Most guests will appreciate the consideration, even if they decline special treatment.

Common Considerations:

Gluten-Free:

- Use potatoes, rice, quinoa, or corn-based dishes
- Choose gluten-free crackers or bread (many great options exist)
- Avoid thickening sauces with flour unless GF-certified

Dairy-Free:
- Use plant-based butter, milks, or oils
- Skip cream-based sauces or make a dairy-free version
- Offer dairy-free desserts (fruit crisp, sorbet, etc.)

Vegetarian/Vegan:
- Include at least one protein-rich plant dish (chili, beans, lentils)
- Use vegetable broth instead of chicken/beef
- Avoid hidden animal products (gelatin, bacon, etc.)

Nut-Free:
- Ask if trace amounts are okay (for pre-made goods)
- Avoid nut-based sauces or toppings
- Always label desserts clearly

How to Label:
Use small tents, tags, or chalkboards to indicate key features:
- "Gluten-Free"
- "Contains Dairy"
- "Vegan-Friendly"
- "May Contain Nuts"

Not only does this show you care—it saves guests from having to ask, and saves you from being interrupted mid-stir.

Cook to Connect, Not to Perform

Remember: the best meals aren't always the most elaborate—they're the ones shared in good company. It's better to have fewer dishes and more presence than to stress over perfection. Nobody remembers if the carrots were under-roasted. They remember that you looked them in the eye and smiled when you handed them a plate.

Let your meal be a reflection of what matters most: nourishment, inclusion, and joy.

9
TABLE SETTING AND DECORATING IDEAS THAT WOW

You've planned the meal, prepped ahead, and are almost ready to welcome your guests—but now comes the part that sets the stage: the table. Whether you're hosting a formal dinner or a relaxed potluck, the way you set your table speaks volumes about your style, your hospitality, and the atmosphere you want to create.

This chapter is about more than just forks and centerpieces. It's about designing a space that makes people feel grounded, cared for, and ready to connect. And you don't need to spend a lot—or even know all the rules—to do it well.

There's just something about a neatly set table...

Why Table Setting Matters (But Doesn't Need to Be Complicated)

We eat with our eyes first. A beautifully set table invites your guests into the moment—it says, "I prepared this for you," even if the food came from the freezer aisle. The good news is, creating that sense of welcome doesn't require perfection or expensive décor. It requires **intention**.

Your table is where everything converges: nourishment, conversation, memory-making. It doesn't have to be fancy to be powerful. In fact, the most meaningful tables are often the simplest. A few thoughtful touches can transform a space, elevate a meal, and create a rhythm your guests will look forward to again and again.

Table-Setting Basics for Any Style of Gathering

Whether you're serving a plated dinner, a buffet meal, or a weekend brunch, having a flexible approach to setting your table can make everything feel more seamless and more special.

Formal Table Settings

These are best for holiday dinners, anniversary meals, or when you want to elevate the experience a bit.

The Basics:
- Charger (optional) underneath dinner plate
- Dinner plate topped with salad plate or soup bowl
- Napkin either beneath forks, on the plate, or in a ring
- Forks to the left (salad outside, dinner fork inside)
- Knife and spoon to the right (knife closest to plate, blade inward)
- Water glass above knife, wine glass to its right
- Place card or menu optional, but a lovely touch

When to Use:

Thanksgiving, Christmas, special birthdays, or when you want to make the meal feel ceremonial.

Casual Table Settings

Ideal for everyday dinners, relaxed weekends, or gatherings with close friends and family.

The Setup:
- Dinner plate, fork, knife, and napkin—done
- Glass for water or a drink of choice
- Optional salad or side plate
- Use placemats or a simple table runner instead of a full cloth

Make It Yours:

Use mismatched plates, hand-drawn name cards, or linen napkins to bring personality without pressure.

Buffet or Self-Serve Settings

The key here is creating flow. You want guests to move smoothly from food to table with minimal confusion.

Buffet Setup Order:

1 Plates (stacked at the front)
2 Mains
3 Sides
4 Condiments and sauces

THE ART OF HOSTING: YOUR HOLIDAY ENTERTAINING... 97

5 Napkins and utensils (at the end or on the tables)

6 Drinks in a separate area, if possible

Tips:

- Label each dish—especially important for dietary clarity
- Use trays, boxes, or upside-down bowls to create height and dimension
- Keep hot items together and use trivets or towels beneath warm dishes

Creating Stunning Centerpieces with Simple Materials

A centerpiece doesn't need to be elaborate or expensive. It just needs to feel intentional and reflect the tone of your gathering. The best centerpieces are low enough to see across and simple enough not to interfere with passing dishes or elbow room.

Seasonal Centerpiece Ideas

Fall / Thanksgiving:

- Small pumpkins, pinecones, eucalyptus garland
- Votive candles in amber glass or small mason jars
- Burlap runner with dried leaves or wheat stalks

Winter / Christmas:
- Evergreen clippings with cranberries or pomegranate accents
  - Clear vases filled with ornaments or fairy lights
  - Taper candles and pine branches on a white tablecloth

Spring / Easter:
- Fresh tulips, daffodils, or hyacinths in simple pitchers
- Pastel eggs in a bowl or scattered with moss and candles
- Linen napkins in soft tones with floral napkin rings

Summer / Fourth of July:
- Bowls of lemons or limes, small herb pots
- Mason jars with daisies or sunflowers
- Striped runners, gingham napkins, or woven placemats

Non-Floral Centerpiece Alternatives
- pitcher can hold wildflowers.
- Candles clustered on a serving tray
- Wooden board with seasonal fruit and greenery
- Decorative bowls with stones, beads, or dried flowers

Budget-Friendly Décor That Brings Any Table to Life
Great style doesn't require a big spend. In fact, many of the most

charming tablescapes are built from thrift store finds, natural elements, and everyday household items.

The "One Theme, Three Touches" Rule

Choose a theme or a dominant color, then reflect it in three ways:
- Table linen or runner
- Centerpiece or floral accent
- Napkins or name tags

This technique creates visual cohesion without buying a full set of coordinated décor.

Budget Décor Sources:
- **Thrift Stores:** Vintage candleholders, platters, fabric remnants
- **Nature:** Pinecones, branches, stones, wildflowers
- **Dollar Stores:** Glassware, chargers, LED lights, faux florals
- **Your Own Home:** Books, jars, baskets, scarves, pitchers

Small Touches, Big Impact:
- Folded cloth napkins (instead of paper)
- A handwritten note or quote at each seat
- Mini favor at each setting (wrapped chocolate, tea bag, sprig of rosemary)
- Candles—real or battery-operated—add instant warmth

Setting the Tone with Style and Presence

A well-set table is more than a backdrop—it's part of the experience. But don't let aesthetics steal your peace. Let it serve your gathering, not overshadow it.

The most beautiful tables are those that reflect the heart behind them. They say:
- "I thought of you."
- "You matter to me."
- "Welcome."

So light a candle. Fold a napkin. Place a sprig of herbs by a plate. And then—let it go. Your presence, your ease, and your warmth are what will truly stay with your guests.

10

DRINKS, TOASTS, AND BAR SETUPS FOR THE HOLIDAYS

The drinks table is often the most underrated part of holiday hosting—and yet, it can quietly set the tone for your entire gathering. A warm mug handed to a guest on arrival, a festive toast before dinner, a self-serve station that makes people feel empowered and relaxed: these are not small details. They are emotional cues that say, "You're welcome here. Help yourself. You're part of this."

This chapter will show you how to confidently and creatively handle everything from signature cocktails to inclusive mocktails, drink station setups, and toast-giving—even if you're not a mixologist or a public speaker. As always, the goal isn't perfection—it's presence, intention, and connection.

The Role of Drinks in Holiday Hospitality

Drinks are the quiet welcome of a party—the first thing you hand a guest when they arrive, the last sip they linger over as the night winds down. They can be celebratory or soothing, bold or delicate, alcoholic or not—but they always say, "Pause here. Settle in."

Why this matters:

• Drinks help set the **pace** of the event: a glass of wine slows things down, a mocktail adds fun, a hot drink creates warmth.

• Offering inclusive drink choices (especially non-alcoholic ones) shows emotional and cultural awareness.

• A thoughtfully set-up bar reduces host workload and allows guests to help themselves, creating comfort and flow.

In short: drinks matter. They're a hospitality tool, not just a menu item.

Holiday Cocktail and Mocktail Recipes

You don't need a stocked bar to offer great drinks. A few simple, seasonal ingredients and a handful of reliable recipes are all you need.

Warm Holiday Favorites
Mulled Wine
• Red wine, orange slices, cinnamon sticks, cloves, honey
• Heat gently on the stove or in a slow cooker
• Garnish with citrus peel or star anise

Spiced Apple Cider (with or without bourbon)
- Apple cider, orange slices, whole cloves, cinnamon sticks, ginger
  - Add bourbon for adult guests or serve as-is for everyone
  - Keeps warm in a slow cooker for hours

Peppermint Mocha (Coffee or Cocoa Base)
- Brewed coffee or hot cocoa, peppermint extract, whipped cream
  - Optional: add Irish cream or peppermint schnapps
  - Garnish with crushed candy canes

Chilled Festive Cocktails

Cranberry Mule
- Vodka, cranberry juice, ginger beer, lime juice
- Serve in copper mugs with ice and fresh cranberries

Holiday Sangria (White or Red)
- Wine, orange liqueur (optional), sliced apples, oranges, pomegranate seeds
  - Stir and chill for a few hours in advance
  - Garnish with cinnamon sticks

Pomegranate Fizz
- Pomegranate juice, sparkling water, lemon juice, simple syrup
- Serve in flutes with a rosemary sprig

Delicious Mocktails

Winter Citrus Sparkler
- Grapefruit juice, soda water, splash of elderflower syrup
- Garnish with thyme or mint

Ginger Sparkle
- Ginger beer, lime juice, cranberry garnish
- Great for those who like bold flavors without alcohol

Cucumber-Mint Cooler
- Cucumber slices, lemon juice, mint leaves, soda water
- Refreshing and easy to make in a pitcher

Every cocktail can have a mocktail counterpart. This isn't just smart hosting—it's inclusive hosting.

How to Set Up a Self-Serve Drink Station

A self-serve station takes pressure off the host and invites guests to take care of themselves in a relaxed way. It also adds a visual and experiential focal point to the room.

The Basics of a Great Drink Station

Choose the Right Spot:
- Sideboard, bar cart, folding table, or kitchen island
- Away from the main food line to avoid crowding

Organize by Flow:

1 Glassware or cups

2 Ice and stirrers

3 Spirits or drink bases

4 Mixers and garnishes

5 Napkins and small plates (if needed)

Add Visual Style:
- Use trays, baskets, or risers for levels and texture
- Small signs or cards labeling drinks and ingredients
- Add candles, garland, or fairy lights for ambiance

Essential Items to Include:
- Glasses (or festive disposables if preferred)
- Ice bucket with tongs or scoop
- Pitchers of mocktails or punch
- Cocktail shaker or mixing spoon
- Garnishes: citrus slices, herbs, berries
- Bar towel for easy clean-up

Kid-Friendly Options:
- **Hot Cocoa Bar:**

Hot chocolate in a slow cooker, marshmallows, whipped cream, sprinkles, crushed candy canes
- **Juice Mocktail Station:**

Apple juice, ginger ale, fruit slices, fun straws, and plastic cups
Label everything so guests feel confident helping themselves.

Giving Great Toasts Without Feeling Awkward

A well-timed toast can turn a good gathering into a memorable one. But many hosts avoid them, afraid of feeling corny or put on the spot. Here's how to make toasting feel authentic—and doable.

When to Toast:
- Just before dinner is served (a welcome and thank-you)
- Before dessert (a moment of reflection)
- At the end of the night (gratitude and closure)
- On New Year's Eve (a look back and forward)

Simple, Warm Toast Templates

Gratitude:

"I just want to say thank you—for coming, for bringing your energy, and for sharing this time. It means a lot to me."

Celebration:

"Here's to the laughter, the learning, and everything we've made it through. May this season bring joy and rest to us all."

Milestone:
"To [guest or event], whose strength and spirit make this day so meaningful. We're so glad to celebrate with you."

Tips for a Great Toast:
- Keep it under 60 seconds
- Speak from the heart, not from a script
- Don't worry about being profound—honest is better than eloquent
- Look at your guests, raise your glass, and invite them to join in

Interactive Toasting Ideas:
- **One-Word Wish:** Have each guest share a word they hope defines their new year
- **Gratitude Jar:** Pull a card from a bowl with anonymous notes of thanks
- **Memory Moment:** Ask everyone to share a favorite moment from the year (great for close-knit groups)

Final Touches That Elevate the Experience

Here are a few last-minute ideas to make your drink service feel polished and inviting:

- **Signature Drink:** Offer one house cocktail or mocktail and pre-fill glasses to serve as guests arrive
- **Printed Menu:** A mini chalkboard or printed recipe card adds a professional touch
- **Seasonal Garnishes:** Cranberries, rosemary, orange slices, cinnamon sticks—visual and aromatic
- **Glass Tags or Wine Charms:** Helps guests keep track of their drinks
- **Drink Coasters or Napkin Stack:** Prevents mess and looks thoughtful
- **Music Near the Bar:** A curated playlist invites guests to linger and chat

. . .

Raise Your Glass, Not Your Stress

Drinks and toasts aren't about presentation—they're about permission. They give people a reason to pause, to savor, to celebrate. You don't have to be an expert bartender or speechwriter. You just have to care—and offer something with love.

So light the candle, chill the cider, warm the mugs, pour with presence. Cheers to the kind of holiday hosting that flows, sparkles, and leaves everyone feeling a little more connected.

PART IV: People, Conversation & Party Dynamics

Hosting isn't just about the food or décor—it's about people. You can have the most beautifully set table and a flawless meal plan, but if your guests feel out of place, disconnected, or uncomfortable, the gathering will fall flat.

This section is your guide to the emotional intelligence side of hosting. It's where logistics meet human dynamics, and where true hospitality lives. These chapters will help you spark connection, blend diverse personalities with ease, and manage awkward moments with grace. Because a successful gathering doesn't come from everything going right—it comes from everyone feeling seen, safe, and welcome.

11

CONVERSATION STARTERS AND ICEBREAKERS THAT ACTUALLY WORK

To help you foster meaningful connection at your gatherings—whether your guests know each other well or are meeting for the first time. This chapter equips you with approachable conversation prompts, low-pressure games, and smart strategies for creating social ease across a mixed group of friends, family, kids, and guests of all kinds.

Why Conversation Matters More Than Small Talk

When people say a gathering "felt good," what they're often describing is connection. Not the food. Not the playlist. Not even the decor. It's the **emotional atmosphere**—and that's shaped by conversation.

But here's the truth: great conversation doesn't always happen automatically. And as the host, you have more power to shape it than you think.

Set Connection as the Goal

Your job isn't to eliminate awkwardness—it's to help your guests move **through** it. The most powerful hosting mindset is this:

"I don't need to impress anyone. I just want people to feel at ease."

Awkward silences aren't failure—they're natural. Especially when you mix people from different backgrounds, generations, or social groups. The trick is not to force conversations, but to **gently guide** them with intention and permission.

Conversation Starters for Every Group

Think of conversation prompts as **on-ramps**—they help people merge into connection without needing to think of the perfect thing to say. These work at the dinner table, around the living room, or during casual mingling.

Light-Hearted & Fun

Use these to break the ice or get laughs flowing:
- "What's the weirdest holiday tradition you've ever seen or done?"
- "If you could teleport anywhere for New Year's Eve, where would you go?"
- "Which dish here would you take to a deserted island?"
- "What was your most memorable birthday gift as a kid?"
- "Which fictional family would you want to join for dinner?"

More Meaningful Prompts

Use these when the energy feels right for deeper sharing:
- "What's one thing you're truly grateful for this season?"
- "What's something small you're looking forward to in the next month?"
- "Was there a moment this year that surprised you (in a good way)?"
- "What's a tradition from your childhood you'd love to revive or reinvent?"
- "What's one thing you're letting go of this year?"

Creative Delivery Tips
- Tuck prompts under plates or fold into napkin rings

- Use a centerpiece bowl where guests can draw questions
- Place one question at each seat with dessert
- Write prompts on leaves, ornaments, or bookmarks for themed décor

Easy, Inclusive Games for Mixed Ages

Sometimes structured interaction makes conversation easier—especially when you've got a range of ages, personalities, or comfort levels in the room.

Here are games that are light, interactive, and require **zero prep**:

Pass-the-Question Bowl
- Fill a bowl with pre-written questions.
- Pass it around during appetizers or dessert.
- Each guest draws one and answers aloud—or picks someone else to answer it.

The "Guess Who" Game
- Before guests arrive, collect one fun fact about each (e.g., "Used to sing in a punk band," "Once met Oprah").
- Read them aloud one by one.

- The group guesses who it is.

2 Truths and a Tradition
- Each guest shares two true things about themselves and one made-up holiday tradition.
- The others try to spot the fake.

Holiday-Themed Charades or Emoji Quizzes
- Create cards with holiday-related words or emojis (e.g., mistletoe, sleigh ride, fruitcake) and act them out.

Group Storytelling
- One person starts a story with one sentence ("It was a snowy night…").
- Go around the room, each person adding one sentence.
- Laughter guaranteed, especially with kids involved.

Pro Tip: Keep games optional and low-stakes. The point isn't performance—it's playfulness.

How to Mix Friend Groups, Family, and Strangers

Blending groups can feel daunting. You might have your coworkers on one end of the table and your cousins on the other. The secret? Help people feel like **they belong**—even if they don't know anyone else.

Make Thoughtful Introductions

Go beyond names:
- "This is Rachel—we met in a book club, and she makes the world's best chili."
- "This is my cousin James. He once fixed a car with duct tape—true story."

Give people conversation hooks in how you introduce them.

Assign a "Friendly Ambassador"

If you're hosting a larger group and know you'll be busy, assign a close friend or extroverted guest to help newcomers feel welcome. Let them know in advance so they can step in naturally.

Use Place Cards with Purpose

Strategic seating can make a world of difference:
- Alternate familiar faces and new connections
- Put high-energy people in conversation anchor spots
- Use cards that double as conversation starters or include fun facts

Create Conversation Zones

Designate small areas where mingling feels natural:
- A drink station with a few stools nearby
- A game table or photo area
- A cozy corner with soft lighting and extra chairs

People connect better when they don't feel like they're on display—give them spaces to land.

You Don't Have to Entertain, You Just Have to Connect

As a host, you are the energy keeper—but not the entertainer. Your job isn't to perform or manage every moment. It's to create an atmosphere of **ease**, where connection can naturally unfold.

With a few light prompts, some playful games, and a little guidance, you'll help strangers become friends—and friends feel like family.

And that? That's the true art of hosting.

12
HOW TO HANDLE AWKWARD GUESTS, FAMILY DRAMA & CONFLICT

Holiday gatherings are often portrayed as joyful reunions filled with laughter and warmth. However, the reality for many is that these occasions can also bring tension, unresolved issues, and challenging dynamics to the forefront. This chapter aims to equip you with strategies to navigate these complexities with grace, ensuring that both you and your guests can enjoy the festivities.mind24-7.com

Setting the Emotional Tone as the Host

As the host, you play a pivotal role in setting the atmosphere of your gathering. Your demeanor, reactions, and energy can influence the overall mood.

a. Embrace Calmness and Positivity

Approach the event with a calm and positive mindset. Your composure can help diffuse potential tensions and encourage guests to mirror your demeanor.

b. Anticipate and Prepare

Reflect on past gatherings to identify potential stressors or conflicts. By anticipating possible challenges, you can prepare responses or strategies to address them effectively.

c. Model Respectful Behavior

Demonstrate respectful communication and active listening. This sets a standard for interactions among guests and fosters a respectful environment.

Boundaries Without Guilt

Establishing boundaries is essential for maintaining your well-being and ensuring a harmonious gathering.

a. Identify Your Limits

Understand your comfort levels regarding topics of conversation, guest interactions, and personal space. Recognizing these limits allows you to set clear boundaries.

b. Communicate Clearly and Kindly

Express your boundaries to guests in a clear yet compassionate manner. For example, if certain topics are off-limits, you might say, "Let's focus on enjoying our time together and steer clear of sensitive subjects."

c. Enforce Boundaries Consistently

If a boundary is crossed, address it promptly and calmly. Reiterate your position and, if necessary, take appropriate action to uphold your limits.

3. Diffusing Tension Before It Escalates

Proactively managing potential conflicts can prevent them from escalating and disrupting the gathering.

a. Monitor Interactions

Stay attentive to conversations and body language. If you notice signs of discomfort or rising tension, intervene subtly to redirect the interaction.

b. Use Neutral Topics as Diversions

Steer conversations towards neutral or light-hearted topics to ease tensions. Discussing shared interests or positive memories can help shift the focus.

c. Provide Private Spaces

Designate areas where guests can retreat for a moment of solitude or to have private conversations. This can be especially helpful for guests who may feel overwhelmed.

When Conflict Does Happen

Despite best efforts, conflicts may arise. Handling them with composure and empathy is key.

a. Stay Calm and Objective

Maintain a calm demeanor and avoid taking sides. Address the issue objectively, focusing on resolving the conflict rather than assigning blame.

b. Offer Mediation

If appropriate, offer to mediate the discussion between conflicting parties. Encourage open communication and mutual understanding.

c. Know When to Step Back

Recognize when it's best to step back and allow individuals space to cool down. Sometimes, giving time can be the most effective way to de-escalate a situation.

Navigating family dynamics and potential conflicts during holiday gatherings requires empathy, preparation, and clear communication. By setting a positive tone, establishing boundaries, and addressing issues with grace, you create an environment where all guests feel respected and valued. Remember, the goal is not perfection but connection and shared joy.

13
HOW TO END A PARTY GRACEFULLY (AND KEEP GUESTS SMILING)

We spend so much energy planning how to *start* a gathering—how to welcome guests, set the tone, break the ice—but rarely do we talk about how to *end* one. And yet, the final moments of a party are some of the most memorable.

How you wrap up a gathering leaves a lasting emotional impression. Done well, it feels like a natural close to a beautiful evening. Done poorly, it can feel rushed, awkward, or abrupt. In this chapter, you'll learn how to master the art of leaving guests smiling, expressing gratitude, and gently reclaiming your space—all while protecting your own energy for a smooth post-party reset.

Why the Ending Is Just as Important as the Beginning

Whether it's a weeknight dinner or a full holiday blowout, guests will likely remember how they felt as they walked out your door. The final 15–30 minutes of a gathering shape that "aftertaste"—it can feel warm and grateful or chaotic and abrupt.

A thoughtful closing signals:
- The event was intentional from beginning to end

- Your guests were appreciated, not just accommodated
- You're a calm, confident host who knows how to manage the energy of the room

Ending well also helps *you*, the host, avoid burnout. It creates closure, prevents lingering exhaustion, and makes the reset easier.

The Art of Wrapping Up Without Rushing Anyone Out

You don't need to declare "the party's over!" to end a gathering well. The key is subtle cues and a gradual shift in energy.

Gentle Closing Signals

- **Shift the mood**: lower the music volume, dim the lights slightly, or switch to softer tunes.
- **Clear a few items**: begin stacking dessert plates or collecting empty glasses—it communicates that things are winding down.
- **Verbally acknowledge the time**: "I can't believe it's already 10—this night flew by!"
- **Invite a final moment**: "Let's have one more toast before everyone heads out."

Sample Phrases to Use

- "Before you go, I want to say thank you—this night meant a lot to me."
- "Let me grab a little something for you to take home."
- "Let's make sure you get leftovers—I'd love to send you with a plate."
- "It's getting late and I know folks have a busy day tomorrow—I'm so grateful you came."

This way, you invite a closing, not enforce one.

Parting Gestures That Leave a Lasting Impression

Small tokens of appreciation can turn a simple goodbye into a cherished memory. These gestures are especially impactful during holidays or milestone events.

THE ART OF HOSTING: YOUR HOLIDAY ENTERTAININ... 119

Thoughtful Ideas
- **Send guests home with food**: Wrap leftovers in reusable containers or foil, labeled with a note.
- **Mini thank-you gifts**: Homemade cookies, a tea bag bundle, a handwritten quote, or even a printed recipe from the meal.
- **Group photo**: Snap a casual photo of everyone and send it the next day with a message of appreciation.
- **Follow-up gratitude**: Send a short text the next day: "So grateful for last night. Loved having you at the table."

These touches reinforce connection and community—and they keep your gathering alive in people's memories well beyond the evening itself.

Quick Post-Party Reset (So You Don't Dread Hosting Again)

One of the biggest sources of hosting dread is what comes *after* the guests leave: the clean-up. But it doesn't have to be overwhelming.

The key is doing a small, strategic reset before bed, and leaving the rest for a calm morning after.

Your 10-Minute Night-Of Reset
1 Load the dishwasher or rinse dishes
2 Wipe counters and tables
3 Toss or refrigerate leftover food
4 Take out trash or recycling
5 Blow out candles or unplug lights

This gets your space 70% reset—without sacrificing rest.

Your Morning-After Ritual
- **Make coffee or tea before anything else**
- **Open windows or light a candle**
- **Put on music or a podcast**
- **Do a slow cleanup while reflecting on the evening**

If you journal, jot down one or two moments you loved—this builds your emotional connection to hosting and turns it into a ritual of joy.

The End Is Part of the Hospitality

How you say goodbye matters. It doesn't need to be grand. It just needs to be intentional.

Hosting is a full arc: the welcome, the gathering, the connection, and the close. Ending a party gracefully ensures your guests feel celebrated until the very last moment—and it gives you, the host, a sense of ease and satisfaction, too.

PART V: THE ENTERTAINING TOOLKIT

These two chapters are designed to be your fallback plan, your creative spark, and your safety net. Whether you're thrown into last-minute hosting or simply prefer to keep things relaxed and resourceful, this part of the book will show you how to host well—with less stress, more joy, and zero perfectionism required.

14

DIY HOSTING HACKS FOR LAST-MINUTE MAGIC

Fast, effective solutions for unexpected guests, short prep windows, or forgotten details—without panic or perfectionism. These ideas prioritize resourcefulness, calm, and joy in the moment.

Pantry Staples for Last-Minute Hosting

When time is tight or guests drop in with little warning, a well-stocked pantry becomes your greatest asset. The goal is not to stock everything—but to keep a small set of reliable, versatile ingredients that can turn into something festive on short notice.

Always-Handy Ingredients

Shelf-Stable Snacks:
- Crackers (plain, seeded, or artisan)
- Mixed nuts or marinated olives
- Jarred artichokes, sundried tomatoes, or pickles
- Jam or honey for cheese pairings

Fridge & Freezer Essentials:
- Cheese (hard and soft), cured meats

- Frozen baguette, naan, or flatbread
- Frozen puff pastry or pie crust
- Butter, eggs, cream

Pantry Staples for Cooking/Baking:
- Pasta, rice, canned beans, canned tomatoes
- Olive oil, vinegar, mustard, garlic
- Flour, sugar, brown sugar, chocolate chips, baking soda

Emergency Dishes from Pantry

5-Minute Dips:
- White bean and garlic spread
- Quick hummus with canned chickpeas
- Cream cheese + jam + crackers

Quick Bakes or Appetizers:
- Pasta tossed with garlic, oil, and chili flakes
- Crostini from sliced toast topped with jarred antipasto
- Puff pastry tarts with cheese and veggies

Last-Minute Dessert:
- Boxed brownie mix dressed with sea salt and olive oil
- Chocolate chip skillet cookie
- Fruit crisp with oats, sugar, butter, and frozen fruit

Quick Decor Upgrades with What You Have

A festive atmosphere doesn't require elaborate decorating—it requires *intention*. Here are ways to make your space feel styled, even if you have only 10 minutes and no budget.

3-Minute Centerpieces

- **Citrus + tea lights**: Place oranges, lemons, or clementines in a wooden bowl and nestle in small candles.
- **Books + flowers**: Stack a few hardcover books and top with a single grocery-store bouquet in a jar or vase.
- **Scarves as runners**: A patterned scarf or fabric scrap down the center of your table adds instant color and softness.
- **Jars of pantry items**: Layer dried lentils, beans, or pasta in glass containers for an earthy touch.

Lighting and Texture Tricks

- Switch off overhead lights and use lamps, string lights, or battery-operated candles.
- Layer blankets and throws on seating areas.
- Add pillows or cushions in unexpected places for instant warmth.

Tabletop Touches

- **Napkin magic**: Fold paper napkins in half with a sprig of rosemary or tie with kitchen twine.
- **Name cards**: Write names on tags, leaves, gift labels, or plain paper tucked into a fork.

- **Mini center items**: Small bowls of nuts, ornaments, or greenery spaced across the table feel intentional.

Instant Menu Enhancements

You don't need to cook everything from scratch to serve something delicious. With a few smart tweaks, you can take store-bought food from basic to beautiful.

How to Make Store-Bought Look Homemade

- **Transfer items to real dishes**: Ditch the packaging—use platters, wooden boards, bowls.
- **Add garnish**: A sprinkle of herbs, lemon zest, or a drizzle of oil transforms frozen or deli items.
- **Use sauces**: Serve a simple store-bought meat dish with a drizzle of balsamic glaze or garlic yogurt sauce.

Reheating Tips

- Re-crisp breads or baked goods in the oven, not microwave.
- Add foil during reheating to retain moisture in casseroles or pasta.

- For meats, splash a little broth or citrus juice before warming.

Signature Drink Shortcuts

Use pantry or fridge basics to create instant drinks:
- Sparkling water + citrus + mint = DIY spritzer
- Ginger beer + lime + cranberry juice = holiday mocktail
- Coffee + Irish cream or flavored syrup = instant festive drink

Wow-Factor Appetizer Board in 15 Minutes

1 Use a large cutting board, platter, or tray.
2 Add crackers, cheese, olives, grapes, nuts.
3 Include one dip (store-bought with olive oil on top).
4 Fill gaps with dried fruit or fresh herbs.
5 Serve with cocktail napkins or toothpicks.

It looks fancy. You spent 10 minutes. Nobody has to know.

Pre-Party Timeline Checklist

A clear to-do list broken into:
- 1 week out
- 2 days out
- Morning of
- 1 hour before
- Just before guests arrive

Menu Planning Grid

Columns for:
- Mains, sides, dessert, drinks
- Who's making what
- Oven/stove timing
- Dietary notes

Grocery & Decor Checklist

Divided by section:
- Pantry, fridge, freezer
- Decor (lighting, centerpieces, place settings)

Dietary Restrictions Tracker
- A guest-by-guest list with allergies, food preferences, and notes

- Meal ideas that accommodate various needs without making five versions

"Oh No!" Fix-It Guide

Quick solutions for:
- Burnt edges or overcooked dishes
- Missing ingredients (with common swaps)
- Forgotten napkins, drinks, or ice

Last-Minute Hosting Flowchart

Feeling overwhelmed? Follow a simple "choose your own adventure" chart:
- "Only 30 minutes?" → App board + signature drink + candlelight
- "No time to cook?" → Order takeout + set the table with style
- "Forgot a gift?" → Handwritten card + leftovers to-go

> *Hosting at the last minute doesn't mean sacrificing connection. It means leading with presence, confidence, and resourcefulness. With a few tools and mindset shifts, you'll begin to see that the magic doesn't come from hours of prep—it comes from creating space for people to feel welcomed.*

15
HOSTING ON A BUDGET: AFFORDABLE CELEBRATIONS THAT SHINE

Hosting beautifully doesn't mean spending extravagantly. In fact, some of the most memorable and meaningful gatherings happen when we get creative within our limits. This chapter is here to help you create magic—even on a modest budget. Whether you're saving for something big, dealing with inflation, or just prefer simplicity, you'll learn exactly where to splurge, where to save, and how to host with confidence and style, without overspending.

Reframing Budget Hosting: The Mindset Shift
Before we dive into tactics, let's bust a myth: Hosting on a budget is not lesser hosting. It's **thoughtful hosting**. It's intentional. And often, it's more meaningful.
Why Less Can Be More:
• Simplicity invites authenticity. When you're not hiding behind grandeur, people connect more easily.
• Constraint fuels creativity. A limited budget encourages you to be resourceful, personal, and original.

- No one remembers how much you spent. They remember how you made them feel.

Common Myths to Release:
- "I need fancy dishes to impress guests." → You need warmth, not Wedgewood.
- "Budget means cheap-looking." → With a few tricks, low-cost can look luxe.
- "Hosting is expensive by default." → It can be, but it doesn't have to be.

Where to Splurge and Where to Save

When budget is tight, being strategic about where to put your money can transform your experience as a host.

Smart Splurges (Buy once, use forever):
- **Good serveware**: A few classic platters or wooden boards elevate everything.
- **Cloth napkins**: Even one set, in a neutral tone, adds elegance and can be reused endlessly.
- **Candles and lighting**: Mood is everything—and a few tea lights go a long way.
- **A signature item**: This could be a signature cocktail glass, a beautiful bowl, or a table runner that becomes your hosting "signature."

Easy Saves:
- **Decor**: Use natural elements (greenery, fruit, branches), dollar-store finds, and what you already own.
- **Drinks**: Serve one or two crowd-pleasing drinks in batches (like sangria or mulled cider), instead of stocking a full bar.
- **Food**: Focus on affordable base ingredients (grains, legumes, veggies) and supplement with small flavor-rich touches (cheese, herbs, sauces).

Rule of Thumb: Spend on tools that you can reuse. Save on anything that disappears after one event.

. . .

High-Impact, Low-Cost Décor and Menu Ideas

When you remove the pressure to dazzle, you make room for impact through simplicity and detail. These ideas prove that budget-friendly can still be breathtaking.

Budget-Friendly Décor

- **Centerpieces from nature**: Pinecones, acorns, bare branches in a vase, citrus with cloves, or fresh herbs tied with string.
- **Use what you have**: Books, scarves, candles, baskets, trays—rethink their placement or purpose.
- **The power of light**: String lights, LED candles, and warm bulbs instantly create ambiance.

- **Printables & handmade details**: DIY place cards, printed menu cards, or folded paper table numbers add a custom feel.

Pro Tip: Pick a *color palette* or *mood theme* (like cozy, woodland, retro, etc.) and unify small touches with it.

Menu Ideas That Stretch the Budget

Affordable Mains:

- Baked pastas (lasagna, baked ziti)
- Roast chicken (cheaper and easier than turkey)
- Hearty veggie-based stews or soups
- DIY taco or baked potato bars

Sides That Shine:
- Seasonal roasted veggies
- Grains with vinaigrette and herbs (farro, couscous, rice)
- Big salads with bold toppings (nuts, seeds, cheese crumbles)

Easy + Elegant Desserts:
- Fruit crisps or cobblers
- Bread pudding with a flavored sauce
- Boxed cake with homemade frosting or layers
- DIY cookie platter using store-bought dough + personalized toppings

Bonus Tip: Stretch expensive ingredients with clever pairings (e.g., a small cheese board with lots of fruit and crackers).

Creative Ways to Host Beautifully Without Breaking the Bank

Even without major funds, you can create unforgettable experiences through creativity, community, and intention.

Make It a Potluck (That Doesn't Feel Disorganized)

Structure helps:
- Assign categories (e.g., "Bring a side dish" or "Bring a dessert to share")
- Use a shared sign-up (Google Doc, app, or paper list)
- Ask guests to bring printed recipes to display—adds a conversation starter!

The key? Curate—not control.

Borrow and Share
- Ask a friend or neighbor if you can borrow extra chairs, platters, or folding tables.
- Host collaboratively: Two families or friend groups can share space, dishes, and responsibilities.

Host a Minimalist Gathering

- **Theme: "One Pot, One Pie"** – Everyone brings one dish or dessert.
- **Host with hot drinks only**: Coffee, tea, cider, and cocoa with cookies
- **Afternoon snack hour** instead of dinner
- **Open-house style**: Drop-in holiday cheer, light snacks only, minimal seating needed

Time It Strategically

- Brunches and afternoon gatherings cost less than full dinners
- A Sunday morning cinnamon roll bar is cheaper than a full Saturday night meal

The essence of hosting is not in what you spend—it's in what you **share**. Your space. Your care. Your attention. Your desire to bring people together.

If you've ever hesitated to host because you thought your home wasn't fancy enough or your budget wasn't big enough, let this chapter be your permission slip.

With intention, creativity, and a few trusted tools, you can host beautifully—and sustainably—for years to come.

CONCLUSION: HOST WITH JOY, NOT STRESS — YOUR NEW HOLIDAY HOSTING MINDSET

Host with Joy, Not Stress: Your New Holiday Hosting Mindset

After everything we've explored together—menus and mindset, décor and delegation, holiday-specific plans and last-minute hacks—this is where we land:

Hosting isn't about getting it all right.

It's about showing up with heart, offering what you can, and inviting others into a space that feels like care.

Let's close this book the same way we hope to close every gathering: not with pressure, but with peace. Not with perfection, but with presence.

Embrace Imperfection (It's the Magic Ingredient)

Perfectionism is the thief of connection.

It whispers that your house has to be cleaner, your dishes fancier, your timing flawless. But the truth is: *no one is coming to inspect your baseboards*. People are coming to feel seen, fed, and welcomed.

If something burns, laugh. If someone's late, pour them a drink. If a kid spills on the tablecloth, congratulations—it's now a story.

The gatherings we remember aren't the ones where everything

looked like a magazine. They're the ones where we felt part of something real.

So next time you start to spiral about how things "should" look or how behind you feel, try this simple reframe:

"I don't need to impress anyone. I want to include everyone."

Build Traditions That Reflect You

The most lasting traditions don't usually start with grand plans. They start when someone says, "We should do this again next year."

Your traditions can be simple:
- A family walk after dinner
- A holiday playlist you add to every year
- Cinnamon rolls every Christmas morning
- Matching socks for Thanksgiving
- A candle lit for someone who couldn't be there

You don't need to inherit your family's exact traditions. And you don't need to adopt anyone else's. This is your chance to build something that reflects your values, your energy, your people.

Tradition, at its best, isn't about repetition for its own sake. It's about connection through continuity. And even one small, consistent ritual—done with care—is enough.

Let Hospitality Become Part of Your Life

Some people think hospitality is a skill you turn on for the holidays. But once you embrace its deeper purpose, you realize: **hospitality is a way of being**.

It can show up in big ways—hosting a holiday meal for twenty. And in small, quiet ones—inviting a neighbor in for tea, sending someone home with leftovers, lighting a candle before dinner.

When you treat hosting as a lifestyle, not a performance, everything softens. You stop striving. You start flowing. You stop hosting "for the show," and start hosting from the soul.

You Are Ready

You've read the chapters. You've gathered the tips. You've probably dog-eared a few pages and had a few moments of "Oh, I could totally do that."

Now comes the best part: **You get to begin.**

Start small. Host something low-pressure. Try one new tradition this season. Use the printable toolkit. Adapt a menu idea. Light the candles. Invite someone in.

And if something doesn't go as planned? Let it be a memory. Let it be enough.

You don't need a bigger kitchen.

You don't need a perfect playlist.

You don't need to be anyone other than who you are, right now.

You just need a little space, a little intention, and a heart that says:

"You are welcome here."

And you, dear reader, are now officially a host who knows how to create joy—without the stress.

Now go make magic. One gathering at a time.

www.ingramcontent.com/pod-product-compliance
Lightning Source LLC
LaVergne TN
LVHW050131080526
838202LV00061B/6464